FINDING YOUR OWN
TRUE NORTH
AND HELPING OTHERS
FIND DIRECTION IN LIFE

Patricia R. Adson, Ph.D.

Type & Archetype Press
Type & Temperament, Inc.

Copyright acknowledgements appear on page 194.

Finding Your Own True North— and Helping Others Find Direction in Life. The Life-Improvement Book for Counselors— and Everyone Else! Copyright © 1999 by Patricia R. Adson, Ph.D. All rights reserved.

Printed in the United States of America. No part of this book may be used or reproduced in any manner whatever without written permission, except for brief quotations embodied in reviews and critical articles. For information inquire of Type & Temperament, Inc., /Type & Archetype Press, P.O. Box 200, Chaska, MN 19035-0200 USA

Type & Archetype books are available at quantity discounts for promotional, or business use. For information, write Type & Archetype Press, P.O.

**Type & Temperament, Inc
P.O. Box 14285
Charleston SC 29422 USA
TelToll-Free 1-(800) IHS-TYPE
info@typetemperament.com**

Type & Temperament, Inc. /Type & Archetype Press website:
http://www.typetemperament.com
or
http://www.typearchetype.com

Cover Design by Elise Hollandsworth

FIRST EDITION

Library of Congress Cataloging-in-Publication Data

Adson, Patricia R.
    Finding your own true north : and helping others find direction in life / Patricia R. Adson. -- 1st ed.
       p.   cm.
   Includes bibliographical references.
   ISBN 1-878-287- 38- 9 (pbk.)
    1. Psychotherapy. 2. Archetype (Psychology)--Therapeutic use. 3. Psychotherapists--Psychology.
   I. Title. II. Title: True north.
   RC480.5.A28 1999
616.89'14--dc21   99-39605
                                                      CIP

987654321

Acknowledgments

This book would not have been possible without the encouragement, support, and inspiration of Carol S. Pearson and Bill O'Hanlon. Carol, chief Journey Guide, created this archetypal theory, and Bill, master of unlimited possibilities, devised the therapeutic means to put the archetypes into action.

In graduate school at the University of Minnesota I was inspired by Frank Wood, whose commitment to all that is good in special education, and Norman Garmezy's, whose research in Project Competence, taught me to look for factors related to success instead of tracking down the etiology of failure. In so doing, they showed me how to find my own path.

I am also deeply indebted to Carol Pearson's "Dream Team;" Eileen and Patrick Howley, Chris Saade, and Deborah Marstellar, all of whom added helpful suggestions and encouragement to this book that has been in progress for so very long.

I add a special thanks to my good friends— therapists and Journey Guides— Sheila Herbert and Janet Hutton Senjem for many years of conversation, companionship and support, not only for this project but also for so many other areas of my life.

My sincerest thanks to my clients who have given me permission to use their stories. I have changed the names and identifying aspects of the clients and therapists I write about to protect their privacy, but they know who they are and they have my deepest respect and gratitude.

And of course, Martin— for everything.

To Martin

CONTENTS

Acknowledgements	3
Dedication	4
Contents	5
Preface	9
Introduction to the first edition	12
Reframing Psychotherapy	12
Going Home the Way You Came: My Journey	13
The Five Responsibilities of a Therapist/Guide	20
Chapter One: Introduction to the Territory	22
The Myth of the Hero's Journey	23
The Three Stages of the Hero's Journey	24
Psychosocial Stages and Psychosocial Tasks	25
The Archetypes of the Hero's Journey	28
Pearson's 12 Key Archetypes	29
Putting It All Together: The Stages of the Journey, Archetypes and Developmental Tasks	32
Summary: Therapy and the Territory of the Hero's Journey	36
Conclusion	38
Recommended Reading	39
Chapter Two: Finding Yourself:	
The Therapist's Journey	40
The 4 Archetypes and Elements of the Preparation of the Therapist	42
Innocent	43
Orphan	44
Wounds	46
The Wounded Healer	47
Caregiver	50
Warrior	51
Dragons	51
The Warrior Within	54

The 4 Archetypes and Elements of the Soul Journey of the Therapist	57
The Call	60
Seeker	61
Lover	62
Creator	64
Destroyer	66
Treasures	68
The 4 Archetypes of the Return: Treasures of the Therapist's Self	69
Ruler	70
Sage	72
Magician	74
Jester/Fool	76
Conclusion	78
Recommended Reading	79
Questions to Lead You on a Self-Guided Journey	80

Chapter Three: Finding the Client — 93

Working with Mary	93
Finding versus Diagnosing	95
The Road to Empathy: Going Where the Client Is— Empathic Listening and Acknowledgment	99
Empathy Skills:	
Whole Body Listening: Being Present with the Client	100
Acknowledgment: Letting Them Know They've Been Found	102
Asking open and honest questions	104
Acknowledge with Possibility	107
Describing the Problem	107
Be specific	108
Draw pictures	109
Make sure you're speaking the same language	109
Listing the Assets: Identifying the Baggage	110
Recommended Reading	113
Summary Chart of Chapter Three	114

Chapter Four: Deciding on a Destination: Finding Out Where the Client Wants to Go — 115

The Goals of the Therapist, the Goals of the Client	116
Essential Techniques for Establishing Goals	117
Who Else Needs to Come Along on This Trip? The Inclusion of Interested Others	125
Identifying Potential Roadblocks	127
Recommended Reading	129
Summary Chart of Chapter Four	130

Chapter Five: Choosing the Proper Means of Transportation — 131

How Are we Going to Get There? The Activities of Psychotherapy

The Process of Applied Archetypal Psychotherapy	132
Indications that the client needs to develop trust and autonomy: Preparation for the journey	134
Indications that the client may be seeking identity and intimacy: The journey	135
Indications that the problem may concern the return: development of integrity and generativity	135
Working With Mary	136
Establishing trust: Awakening the Caregiver	137
Encouraging autonomy: Awakening the Warrior	141
Awakening Mary's Warrior	141
Matching Intervention to Client and Situation: Three Depressed Clients	143
Recommended Reading	148
Summary Chart of Chapter Five	149

Chapter Six: Following the Rules of the Road	153
The Professional Journey Guide	153
The nature of professionalism: Therapy is not a social event	153
Maintain a flexible therapist-client relationship	155
Determine who the client is	158
Therapy and society	158
How to Keep Ourselves From Getting Lost	160
Supervision	160
Self-supervision	161
Client supervision	162

Continuing education	162
Recommended Reading	164
Summary Chart of Chapter Six	165

Chapter Seven: Applying the Archetypal Model: Working with Innocents and Orphans — 166

Working with Innocents: the story of Ruth	168
Return to the Innocent	168
Lost and found: The client isn't the only one who can get lost	169
Losing the client	170
Looking at theories instead of facing facts	173
Re-finding the therapist's self	173
Returning to Ruth: The Innocent	173
The trance of the Innocent	175
Casting the spell	176
The archetypal trance	176
Breaking the trance	177
Back to Ruth: Breaking the therapist's trance	178
The therapist's lesson	179
Therapeutic activities: establishing trust and autonomy	179
Therapy notes	181
Facing the fall	182
Assignment in the here and now	183
Destination	183
Working with Orphans: Preparing Mary for the Journey	185
How not to be a politically correct therapist: Refinding ourselves	186
Learning Another Lesson with Mary the Orphan	187
Establishing Trust	189
Relationship of therapist to client	189
Therapeutic activities—Being in the body	191
Summary	193

Copyright Permissions	194
End Notes	195
References	210
About the Author	215

PREFACE

> THE IDEA THAT EVERYONE IS A HERO WITH A UNIQUE GIFT CAN RADICALLY CHANGE THE WAY WE LIVE AND WORK.
> Carol S. Pearson

Each person is a unique individual. Hence psychotherapy should be formulated to meet the uniqueness of the individual's needs, rather than tailoring the person to fit the Procrustean bed of a hypothetical theory of human behavior.
Milton H. Erickson

Psychotherapy is a fluid and fleeting process, difficult to quantify, to describe, or to teach. It is an experience modified continually by the demands of the moment rather than one guided by standard procedure. As a science psychotherapy is new and built on shaky grounds, but as an art it is as ancient as the oldest of myth and story.

As I tried to reconcile the art and the science of psychotherapy I felt lost. Choosing the right path is difficult when each path may lead in a different direction. For years I had followed the paths of others who claimed to have found the right way until gradually their certainties became my uncertainties. I found something useful in almost every theoretical school and configuration in which psychotherapy is practiced. Nevertheless, I continued to seek a common thread or a sound theoretical basis on which to determine the best approach or technique to use selectively.

I found what I was looking for in the context and conceptual vocabulary of the myth of the hero's journey as depicted in the work of Carol S. Pearson. In *Awakening the Heroes Within: Twelve Archetypes to Help Us Find Ourselves and Transform Our World,*[1] Pearson describes the relationship of the hero's journey to the therapeutic process. The word hero, in this context, identifies the ordinary person who is free to choose and capable of change. The task of the hero is the task of claiming one's own life and place in the world instead of having one's life and place in the world determined by others. The journey takes the hero from dependence to independence and ultimately to interdependence and provides a framework for the therapeutic process by presenting these stages of human development in narrative form. Within the myth of hero's journey there is complexity enough to encompass both the unique and the universal in every client's life.

I use Pearson's theoretical construct as the *context* into which a variety of therapeutic techniques and perspectives (the *process* of therapy) can be integrated. In this framework, the role of the therapist is that of a *guide.* The therapeutic approach and goals are tailored to the stage of the client's journey and the unique attributes and personal history of the client. Therapeutic methods are not determined by the particular school or the theoretical model of the therapist. The guide brings to the therapeutic encounter a knowledge of human development, experience in the use of therapeutic techniques to effect change, a personal philosophy centered on respect for the client, and a firm belief that the client has, *within,* the ability and most of the resources needed to change.

To view people who seek psychotherapy as heroes on a life journey requires therapists to broaden the scope of the practice of psychotherapy from one that focuses on a theory of personality, pathology, cognition, or systems, to a focus on the whole human condition: the mind, body, soul, and social responsibility of each client. With this shift in world view — from disease to transition — from part to whole — the role of the therapist changes. And, with the taking on of this new role the therapist's journey begins.

INTRODUCTION

Therapy is what we say it is, i.e., what names we operate with, what explanatory principles we use, and what reality we thereby create.

Paul Watzlawick

Naturally a doctor must be familiar with the so-called methods. But he must guard against falling into any specific, routine approach. In general one must guard against theoretical assumptions. To my mind, in dealing with individuals, only individual understandings will do. We need a different language for every patient. In one analysis I can be heard talking the Adlerian dialect, in another the Freudian.

Carl Jung, *Memories, Dreams, and Reflections*

Re-framing Psychotherapy

A technique often used in family therapy is called re-framing. When re-framing the therapist asks the family to consider a person or a situation in a new light in the hope that by altering their viewpoint the family will change their behavior toward that person.[1] For example, if I ask parents to consider their adolescent son's misbehavior as a striving for independence they might interact differently with him from the way they reacted when they viewed him as a disobedient child. By changing perspective, and looking at their son from *his* point of view rather than *theirs* they could change their attitude and consequently their behavior toward that child.

In this book I ask therapists to re-frame the way they

view their relationship with their clients. I ask therapists not to consider clients as medical patients who have something wrong with them, or as people who are thinking erroneously, or as clients whose symptoms serve some purpose in the family system. Instead, I ask them to consider clients as heroes on a journey; that is, as people who *may* have a problem inside of them or *may* be thinking erroneously or *may* be trying to maintain homeostasis in a system. But, in spite of (or in addition to) all of those other considerations, I ask them to think of clients as people who are on a series of journeys through life, and as people who have the capacity to awaken the inherent inner resources they need in order to continue their journeys and claim their own lives. I reconsider the definition of psychotherapy and think about therapists not as experts, analysts, physicians, or teachers, but as a type of a Journey Guide: a combination of all of the above.

Going Home the Way You Came: My Journey

I came to this place after a journey that took many twist and turns. Early in my training I was part of a supervision group in which one of the trainees attempted to memorize the rules about doing therapy. Each time Colleen brought a case to supervision she asked everyone present how she should handle this particular client. Members of the group, and the supervisors, would oblige her by answering her questions and telling her how to proceed. Because members of the group followed different theoretical models, Colleen often got inconsistent advice. Nevertheless, after each response she nodded and carefully wrote down every suggestion in her ever-expanding notebook. (I pictured her at home each night making lists and drawing arrows and trying to find the proper way to respond to each situation.) At the end of each supervision session Colleen concluded that she should refer the client to someone else because she "really wasn't experienced enough to handle a case like that." Colleen was sure that the answers lay "out there" and that there was a proper treatment for every situation. She remained tentative, and so unsure of herself that she didn't dare make a move that wasn't sanctioned by some authority. Colleen wanted so desperately to do the right thing at all times that she never got around to doing therapy.

For a long time, although I didn't admit it, I felt like Colleen. I wanted someone to give me a map to go by because I wasn't sure what I was supposed to be doing with each client in each situation. Ultimately, however, the more I learned about different theoretical orientations the more I realized that there were many ways to approach any given problem. Nonetheless, I wanted someone to tell me when or how I should select a particular approach: to tell me how to determine which "language" to speak to which client. I felt as if I were "flying by the seat of my pants," and I was uneasy relying on intuition rather than a sound theoretical basis for determining what to do when and with whom.

Concerned about my uncertainties, I began to retrace my steps, hoping to learn from my mistakes by reflecting on what my clients had taught me. I felt compelled to write down what I'd learned — to say it out loud — claiming that I hoped others might learn from my mistakes, but knowing that I was writing so I would understand it myself.

I didn't start out to become a psychotherapist. I began my professional life as a high school social studies teacher. After a few years I stopped teaching and stayed at home to raise five children. When I was ready to return there were no jobs open in my field. The only jobs available were in a new field called special education. Consequently, I went back to school and prepared myself to teach students described as learning disabled, and those labeled "emotionally disturbed and behavior disordered," and in this process I discovered an essential difference between regular and special education.

As a social studies teacher I had been required to submit lesson plans each week. In these plans I outlined the material I was going to cover and listed general goals and specific objectives for each course I taught. The material, the goals, and the objectives were the same for every student. Every student was given the same material in the same way; every student used the same text; and every student was evaluated by the same criteria. As a high school teacher, I had to know a lot about the *subject matter*, a little about teaching methods, and not very much about the students.

In special education I found an emphasis on the specific nature of each student rather than the subject matter. Special education is based on the premise that children with special needs (learning disabilities, emotional problems, physical handicaps, or developmental delays) require Individual Educational Plans based on the specific attributes of the child in question and not on a diagnostic or descriptive label. The diagnosis, or comparison of each child to a statistical norm, qualified a child for special programming but did not, in itself, indicate the specific nature of that programming. The *ideal* in special education was that each child would be considered, not as a statistic, but as an "N of one," and the challenge to the teacher was to find the requisite teaching methods to utilize and bring forth resources within each student: to focus on assets rather than liabilities (and disabilities). I found then that in addition to a mastery of the *subject matter*, I also needed to be familiar with an array of *teaching techniques*, and to learn how to become an expert on each *child*.

Because I was preparing to work with children who had difficulty learning and behaving — children described as disturbed and disturbing— I had to study the psychological theories that sought to explain how these children's difficulties developed. There were theories that placed the problem within the child, and theories that placed the problem in the family system, and theories that placed the problem in the environment. I studied Behavioral Psychology, Psychodynamic Psychology, Ecological Psychology, Cognition, and Systems theory. I learned about complexes, repression and regression, attachment theory, and learning theory — a bewildering array of personality theories each with beautiful explanations as to the causes of the students' problems.

However, once I entered the real world of the classroom I found that the best way to handle any problem wasn't necessarily related to a particular explanation of how the problem developed. Rather, most of the time a combination of many techniques derived from different theories worked better than any techniques derived from one theoretical construct.

From that experience I learned to *start with the child and not the theory;* to start where we were; to gather the necessary information by observation and testing of relevant domains; to reach the child so that he or she would know that we were working together; to develop practical, reachable goals; and to get students involved in the process of learning what they needed to get along in this world so that other people would not have to take care of them for the rest of their lives.

In that setting I also had to determine what was required of *me* in relationship to my students, for I soon realized that my job required more than a love of children. I had to respect and affirm each child's feelings, while simultaneously teaching that child how to behave in concert with others. I needed good judgment to set limits, and not allow children to harm themselves or others. Most important, I had to claim my own authority, and understand my responsibility to each child, to others in the classroom, to the school community, and to the world at large. Now, as a special education teacher, I needed to know about the *subject matter*, the *teaching methods*, the *child*, and about *myself*.

What I learned about myself led me to return again to graduate school for I felt a deep need to be able to work with students in the context of their families and the worlds in which they lived outside of the classroom. I knew that I would need more than teaching credentials to do this and decided to become a psychotherapist.

Again I faced the same array of psychological theories, but now each theory or school of psychology also had its own requirements about relating to the client and specified the therapeutic techniques to be used. For a time I forgot what I had learned as a teacher and tried to follow the paths of others who seemed to know so much more than I. I reverted to the lesson plan approach and once again studied more about the subject matter, whether it was family therapy or cognitive therapy or psychodynamic therapy, than I did about the client. I had gone from theory to experience, and ignoring my experience, was captured once more by theory.

In my search for the perfect theory I read, went to workshops, studied cognitive therapy, clinical hypnosis, solution-oriented, brief, action-oriented and competency-based therapies. I believed that if only I could learn one more technique, take one more course, or read one more book I would find the right way. At the same time, however, I continued to seek a way to consider clients in the context of their own lives; to work, not only with the inner or cognitive lives of clients, but also with the problems of families who were trying to sustain relationships, and the social problems of violence, addictions and abuse.

At last I found the work of Carol Pearson who, building on the theories of Joseph Campbell, correlated the stages of the hero's journey with the developmental stages of dependence, independence and interdependence. This developmental metaphor, a recapitulation of the natural history of the human species, provides a rich context for psychotherapy and a way in which to integrate many therapeutic modalities into a client-centered approach to psychotherapy. It is a structure large enough to include matters of body, mind, soul and social responsibility and legitimate psychotherapeutic concerns.

Now that I had a *context* I needed to re-think the actual *process* of psychotherapy. I wanted a framework in which to place each of the therapeutic activities. I sought a rationale for choosing each therapeutic activity and a way to chart the course of the therapy and keep track of the progress or lack of it. I found that framework in the parallel to my experience as a special education teacher. And, although I knew that teaching and psychotherapy were not the same thing, I could see that they followed the same process. In the context of the hero's journey, my clients were heroes on a journey, their own special journey, and I was their guide. As a special education teacher I had been a guide to each student on an educational journey. In that capacity I had to know everything I could about each student, be familiar with an array of teaching techniques, understand the subject matter and know myself and my role with respect to my students. As a guide in psychotherapy, the *process* was much the same.

Therefore, when I re-cast the client as hero on a journey, I expanded my concept of my role as a therapist to include all I had learned before as a teacher and found that I could use my experience to chart a highly individualized course for each client. Now I could determine my relationship to a client, or choose a therapeutic activity, not by the rules of the therapeutic school I belonged to, but according to the *task* I was trying to accomplish at that moment. Just as I had once considered each student as an "N of one," and designed Individual Educational Plans accordingly, I could now do the same for every client. Therefore, I re-defined the duties of a therapist/guide as listed in the box on the next page:

The Five Responsibilities of a Therapist /Guide

1) Finding Yourself: Training, therapeutic perspective and personal therapy

Knowing where you stand so you can design a proper professional relationship with the client and help clients find their own paths, not yours.

2) Finding the Client: Assessment and Diagnosis

Going where the client is in order to experience the world as he or she does; finding the place on the map where each client is.

3) Deciding on a Destination: Treatment planning and setting goals and objectives

Determining where clients need to go and specifying how they will know when they get there.

4) Choosing the Proper Means of Transportation: Therapeutic interventions

Selecting the therapeutic activity that will best enable the client to reach the specific destination he or she has chosen.

5) Obeying the Rules of the Road: Ethics and continuing education

Maintaining the ethical and educational requirements of your profession and being conscious of your own responsibility to your clients and to society.

When I see my obligations from this viewpoint I can select elements of different schools and types of therapy that will best help me in the performance of each of these tasks. I can use the warmth and genuine regard fostered by Carl Rogers and Humanistic psychologists to find clients and to acknowledge their plight. I can use Solution oriented, family therapy and behavioral techniques to describe problems, decide on a destination, measure progress and to access inherent capacities (archetypes). I can combine the concept of developmental stages and tasks (from developmental psychology) with concepts from archetypal psychology to form a basis on which to choose the proper means of transportation. From Existential psychology I can find ways to consider my clients' questions of meaning encountered on the soul journey. There are times, too, when the best way to get a client to a destination requires first a DSM-IV (American Psychiatric Association Diagnostic and Statistical Manual of Mental Disorders, Fourth Edition, 1994)[2] diagnosis and, possibly, the use of appropriate medication. And there are other times when I have to leave my office to go out and work together with the legal system, the school system, social services, or anyone else who can help my client.

These five tasks are neither discrete nor necessarily sequential and they often overlap. At times the assessment process itself is an intervention. Like any complex task, the art of psychotherapy requires us to do several things at once. In the learning process, however, we have to acquire these skills one at a time.

Before we start any journey, however, we must first study a map of the territory. We begin, therefore, with an overview of the hero's journey concept, and an introduction of the elements of the journey as they relate to the process of psychotherapy. Next we will learn to find direction for ourselves as therapists by taking a personal journey, and finally, we will demonstrate ways to put theory into practice and guide our clients to their own True North.

CHAPTER ONE

Introduction to the Territory: The Hero's Journey, Archetypes and Developmental Tasks

In classical myth, the health of the kingdom reflected the health of the King or Queen. When the Ruler was wounded, the kingdom became a wasteland. To heal the kingdom, it was necessary for a hero to undertake a quest, find a sacred object, and return to heal or replace the Ruler.
    Carol S. Pearson, *Awakening the Heroes Within*

Hero myths originating from different cultures are similar because our psychological progress through life is similar, whether we were reared in New York, or belong to the Netsilik Eskimos; whether we live in the twentieth century or the fifth century before Christ.
    Anthony Storr, *Jung*

In choosing the Oedipus myth, Freud told us less which myth was the psyche's essence than that the essence of psyche is myth, that our work is mythic and ritual, that psychology is ultimately mythology, the story of the stories of the soul.
    James Hillman, *The Myth of Analysis*

The Myth of the Hero's Journey

The myth of the hero's journey is told in many variations from the legends of Parsifal and the Fisher King to the Native American stories of the Vision Quest. In the myth the hero heeds a call (or has a fall from a state of innocence) that impels him or her to leave home, go off to slay dragons, find a gift or a treasure, and return to share that treasure with the community.

The story of the hero's journey is a metaphorical way to consider human developmental processes — the natural history of our species. Human beings are protected by parents or caregivers while we develop the skills to live in the world independently (*prepare to separate*). We go forth in early adulthood to discover our true identity (*the journey inward to discover who we are*) then return to take our places and play our parts in the community or society in which we choose to live (*the return*).

Using this developmental myth as a context in which to consider the psychotherapy client we depart from the familiar analogies of the physical sciences and borrow the analogy from the social sciences that constructs the developmental process as separation, transition, and reincorporation.[1] According to that model, human growth is a process that requires separating repeatedly from the familiar, venturing into the unknown, and returning with new skills and knowledge that enhance both the self and the community at large.

In this context the name "hero" does not connote the conquering hero, or the heroic ego, or even the masculine hero, but harks back to the original meaning of the word that defined a hero as a person who was free to choose in a community of equals rather than a person who was the property of others such as a slave (or in those days, a woman)[2]. Today, every adult can have the potential to be a hero. Because we consider heroes in the context of their entire lives and the society in which they live, we can justify including matters of mind, body, soul and society as legitimate therapeutic concerns. We belong to a social species.

The Three Stages of the Hero's Journey

The hero's journey has three parts; the *preparation,* the *soul journey,* and the *return.* These correspond to the human developmental stages of dependence, independence and interdependence, and to the psychological constructs of the ego, the soul, and the self.[3] That is, we grow from a state of dependency to develop the ego strength needed to live in the world with others. Next, we delve into matters of the soul to discover what makes us unique and at the same time a part of all existence. And at last we arrive at a sense of self that includes both ego and soul and yet is capable of being aware of matters of ego and soul, and at the same time, conscious of the part one plays in the larger society in which one lives. To summarize:

Stage One: Ego Building:
Preparation for Separation— Dependence
Elements: The Call, the Fall, Wounds, Facing the Dragons

Stage Two: The Journey Inward to Find the Individual's Independence— Soul Finding
Elements: Fighting the Dragons and Finding the Treasure

Stage Three: The Return to Community—Interdependence or Responsibility for Self and to Others
Elements: Sharing the Treasure with Others

Psychosocial Stages and Psychosocial Tasks

The psychosocial stages devised by Erik Erikson[4] are the mileposts on the hero's journey that mark the path of human development from childhood to adulthood and onward into later life. At each stage of the journey —dependence, independence, and interdependence — the hero must accomplish specific developmental tasks implicit in that psychosocial stage. Although Erikson considered these stages to be pertinent only to ego development, in the context of the hero's journey the stages pertain to the concepts of soul and self as well. These multidimensional stages are descriptive of the entire range of development: physical, mental, spiritual and social.

Moreover, although the stages are interrelated and sequential, our experience as therapists, educators, and human beings has taught us that each stage does not have to be accomplished in the *life* stage proposed by Erikson (see chart below). From the viewpoint of archetypal psychology we can see that it is possible to accomplish the unfinished business of childhood and adolescence in later years, and that it is neither necessary (nor possible) to return to childhood or ask our parents or others to complete these stages for us. That is, although trust and autonomy must be developed before a person can achieve a sense of identity, it is possible to develop trust and autonomy in later life. Indeed, many of us are well into mid-life before we really know who we are and what we want to do when we grow up. The unfinished business of childhood can be completed in the therapeutic process.

Because psychosocial stages represent common elements of development they comprise a map of the territory traveled by every hero. At each psychosocial stage there is something a client has to learn to do differently or some essential, innate quality that needs to be developed or awakened. What we, as therapists, can do is find a way to help clients accomplish unfinished developmental tasks and, in so doing, activate the inner resources they will need in order to resolve similar issues in the future. To assist in the accomplishment of developmental tasks, we turn for help to the archetypes, the inherent inner resources of "deep and abiding patterns in the human psyche that remain powerful and present over time." [5]

Erikson's Psychosocial Stages[6]

Infancy:	Trust vs. mistrust
Early childhood:	Autonomy vs. doubt and shame
Preschool:	Initiative vs. guilt
School age:	Industry vs. inferiority
Adolescence:	Identity vs. role confusion
Young adulthood:	Intimacy vs. isolation
Middle age:	Generativity vs. stagnation
Later life:	Integrity vs. despair

The Three Stages of the Journey and Erikson's Psychosocial Stages and Tasks

Preparation: Ego development—dependence/trust

Trust	task= developing trust in self and others
Autonomy:	task= standing up for, protecting and defending the self
Initiative:	task= learning to take responsibility for self
Industry:	task= learning basic social skills and work habits

Journey: Soul— identity/independence

Identity:	task= finding what you love, creating, and letting go
Intimacy:	task= finding whom you love, willingness to commit and let go

Return: Self— wholeness/interdependence

Generativity:	task= actively sharing your gifts with others
Integrity:	task= being true to yourself and claiming your own wisdom

The Archetypes and the Hero's Journey

The idea of archetypes is an ancient one. It is related to Plato's concept of ideal forms: patterns already existing in the divine mind that determine in what form the material world will come into being. But we owe to Jung the concept of the psychological archetypes: the characteristic patterns that pre-exist in the collective psyche of the human race, that repeat themselves eternally in the psyches of individual human beings and determine the basic ways that we perceive and function as psychological beings.

Robert Johnson, *Inner Work*[7]

Freud based his theory of personality development on the mother-father-child triad as told in the myth of Oedipus. He believed that a child came into the world as a blank slate whose personality was shaped, developed, and often scarred, by sexually charged events in the relationship of child to parent. To Jung, however, the Oedipus myth was only one aspect of the story. Although Jung agreed that personal experience played a *part* in the development of each individual, he also believed that all humans came into the world with "a common psychic substrate" and that "the essential role of personal experience was to *develop what is already there,* to actualize the archetypal potential already present in the psychological organism, to activate what is latent or dormant in the very substance of the personality, to develop what is encoded in the genetic makeup of the individual..."[8]

That is, Jung believed that humans have certain innate inner constructs that he called archetypes, that are part of every individual and also part of the collective unconscious we all share. Jung concluded that archetypes were activated or awakened by personal experience. It is on that premise that this book is based. When therapists view each person as a creature of innate potential who has the possibility to overcome the limitations of family and culture and become a unique human being, we can help our clients take heroic journeys and find the selves that they were meant to be, rather than having to accept the selves imposed on them by family or society. We can teach our clients how to activate the capacities they were born with, rather than how to contend all their lives with the limitations of the parents they were born to.

Pearson's 12 Key Archetypes

We are aided on our journey by inner guides, or archetypes, each of which exemplifies a way of being on the journey. Each has a lesson to teach us, and presides over a stage of the journey.

Carol S. Pearson

Carol S. Pearson made it easier for us to work with the elusive concept of archetypes by personifying the archetypal images essential to the human developmental process. Pearson called these archetypes inner Journey Guides who are available to guide each hero through the three stages of the journey. She described three levels of each archetype, identified a shadow form, named the gift each archetype brings, and the task it can help us accomplish.[9]

The archetypes are innate predispositions, available to everyone regardless of personal history. However, they may appear to each of us a little differently, clothed as they are in the garb of our culture and personal experience.[10] These inner resources are available at each stage of the journey to help us accomplish life's essential tasks and find the path that leads to our own true

North. Because the archetypes are complex and interrelated, we refer to the archetype as being available to us in higher or lower levels. The highest level of the archetype represents the gift that it brings when it is fully present and integrated with all of the other archetypes of development. The low level or shadow archetype describes the negative side of the archetype when its presence is denied or its characteristics are not tempered by others.

The chart on the next page is a brief introduction to Pearson's archetypes. We will become better acquainted with them later as we take ourselves on a therapist's journey. Later we will also become even more familiar with the multidimensional nature of these archetypes by learning how we, as therapists, acting in the role of external Journey Guides, can awaken and activate in our clients and ourselves the universal forms Pearson called by the familiar names of Innocent, Orphan, Warrior, Caregiver, Seeker, Lover, Destroyer, Creator, Ruler, Magician, Sage, and Fool.

Brief Descriptions of Pearson's 12 Archetypes

1. Archetypes of the Preparation Stage of the Journey

The Innocent: the pure and trusting part of us who retains faith regardless of personal experience.
The Orphan: the part that has been betrayed, abused or abandoned.
The Caregiver: the ability to nurture and care for others and ourselves.
The Warrior: the ability to protect and defend ourselves and set limits and goals.

2. Archetypes of the Soul Journey

The Seeker: the need to search for something different, seek meaning, explore and wander.
The Lover: the ability to care, to bond, to make commitments and to have passion.
The Creator: the ability to open the imagination and bring forth something that never existed before.
The Destroyer: the ability to choose to let go and rid ourselves of things that no longer support our values; also, the acceptance of mortality.

3. Archetypes of the Return

The Ruler: the ability to use all of our resources and to take responsibility for ourselves and for others.
The Sage: the ability to attain wisdom, to seek truth and to tolerate ambiguity.
The Magician: the ability to change what needs to be changed by acting on our own visions.
The Fool: the ability to experience life fully and to tell the truth with impunity.[11]

As this chart demonstrates, people are not archetypes, although at times they may be expressing only one archetype and seem like stereotypes: the victim, the naive, the villain, or the martyr. This can change very rapidly for archetypes are not immutable traits. When I refer to clients as Innocents or Orphans, I am describing people who have not yet prepared themselves for the journey by activating other archetypal resources. In later chapters we will see how this can be done.

Putting It All Together: The Stages of the Journey, Archetypes and Developmental Tasks

Stage one— preparation for the journey: trust and autonomy

"...human beings are born fourteen years too soon. No other animal endures such a long period of dependency on its parents. And then, and suddenly the child is expected to become an adult, and his whole psychological system, which has been tuned and trained to dependency, is now required to respond to the challenges of life in the way of responsibility."
Joseph Campbell, *Myths, Dreams, and Religion*[12]

Young or old, male or female, the preparation for the journey involves learning to be one's own mother and father and there is very little in our culture that encourages us to do so. Preparing for the journey involves learning to become autonomous and learning to have trust in our own ability to take care of ourselves. To prepare for the journey we awaken the archetypes of the Caregiver and the Warrior who become the internal parents who nurture and protect the Orphan and the Innocent.[13]

> Mary slumps in her chair. Her face is barely visible behind her long blonde hair. She stares at the floor and says in a low voice," I just don't want to live like this any more, but why should I think you can help me? No one else has ever been able to. Everyone else has abandoned me."
> Mary, the Orphan, unprepared for the journey.

A journey begins with a call or a fall. The therapeutic journey begins when the client realizes that something is wrong. She feels disillusioned or betrayed, fearful, depressed or anxious (the fall) and suffers the effects of trauma, abuse or abandonment. She may experience wounds inflicted by others as psychological symptoms of depression, anxiety or dissociation and set out to find someone to take care of her, or to fix what is wrong. Clients don't appear on our doorsteps saying they have suffered a fall or heard a call to the journey. They appear stunned by betrayal, numbed by trauma, depressed, anxious, confused, alienated, lost, and, more often than not, needing emergency first aid before they can depart for the journey. The therapist's job is to *find* these lost clients — go where they are and see the world through their eyes — and teach them to protect and care for themselves in preparation for their journeys.

Stage two— the soul journey: identity and intimacy

Each in his lifetime is in the process of bringing forth a specimen of humanity such as never before was made visible upon this earth, and the way to this achievement is not along anyone else's path who ever lived.

Joseph Campbell

When we honor our peculiarities, the process of personal transformation allows us to become all that we might be.

Sheldon Kopp

Celebrate your weirdness.

Bill O'Hanlon

Having learned to survive without parents (or in spite of parents) the hero begins the soul journey, traveling inward to discover his or her own identity — the character and calling that are uniquely his own — instead of accepting those assigned by others. We do this by freeing ourselves from other people's expectations and labels (slaying the dragon), and going within to find our singular resources and abilities (treasures). Once identity has been established, true intimacy is possible, for only when we have accepted all the parts of ourselves can we truly accept another and not expect that other to take care of us.

Paul wrings his hands and speaks slowly and deliberately, "I'm feeling alienated and adrift. I don't seem to have anything in common with my colleagues. I am not sure I should have become a minister."

Paul, the Seeker who may have to leave his church to find his soul.

The therapist's duty at this stage is to be a companion to clients on inner journeys; to show clients how to enter the inner worlds of imagination, dreams, fantasy and symbol, and then how to return, intact, to the world they share with others. The archetypes of the soul that Pearson calls the Seeker, the Lover, the Creator and Destroyer, enable us to discover who we are and what it is that we are called to do; to accomplish the developmental tasks of finding an identity and developing the capacity to commit and to sustain intimacy. The therapist is *no longer acting as a parent but is now a true guide,* one who has traveled her own path and is well acquainted with the territory of inner worlds, but who also knows that heroes must find their treasures themselves. The duty of the guide is to show heroes where to look. The balance between leading and following is a delicate one.

Stage three— the return: integrity and generativity

Your actions matter and you have a responsibility to change the world around you.
Mihaly W. Csikzentmihaly

We must learn to understand ourselves fully without becoming preoccupied only with ourselves.
Sheldon Kopp

In the heroic myths the journey is never over until the hero returns, but only recently have psychotherapists begun to acknowledge social responsibility as a legitimate area of therapeutic concern.[14] Clients bring us many problems involving their relationship to the outer world and, in turn, the disarray of the outer world can be the source of psychological symptoms for clients and ourselves. Those clients whose difficulty lies in taking responsibility for themselves and others, and those who need to change the way in which they interact with the social order are dealing with the problems of the return.

> Gregg winces as he eases awkwardly into his chair. His arthritis is gradually crippling him. Tears brim in his eyes, "I hate my job, I hate my boss. I want to move to a warmer climate, but if I do I won't be able to take part in raising my sons. My ex-wife won't let them come to stay with me for any length of time. I might lose them. I have to choose."
> Gregg, the Ruler, unsure of his kingdom

At the return stage the therapist's duty is to acknowledge and validate the clients' obligations to accept moral responsibility for themselves in the world. In doing this we help them find a way to achieve integrity and generativity by awakening the archetypes of the Ruler, the Sage, the Magician and the Fool. At this stage we sometimes become agents of society or show clients how to call on their inner resources in order to access resources in the outer world. Here, too, we as therapists, have to take responsibility for achieving and maintaining our own professional integrity and generativity.

Summary: Therapy and the Territory of the Hero's Journey

Shifting my focus from a model of disease to one of transition, from a focus on the theory to a focus on the client, I found that I could fit the therapy to the individual client, rather than to the problem, disease, or condition by:
1. determining the stage of the journey on which the client's problem is found,
2. specifying the developmental tasks related to that stage,
3. identifying the archetypal energies needed to accomplish this task, and
4. choosing a therapeutic activity to awaken the archetype in that particular client.

Stages of the Journey and Erikson's Psychosocial Stages/Tasks

Preparation: Ego development— dependence

<u>Archetypes</u>　　　<u>Tasks</u>

Innocent　　　　　trust
Orphan　　　　　　autonomy
Caregiver　　　　　industry
Warrior　　　　　　initiative

Journey:　　Soul— identity/ independence

<u>Archetypes</u>　　　<u>Tasks</u>

Seeker　　　　　　identity
Lover　　　　　　 intimacy
Creator
Destroyer

Return:　　Self— wholeness/ interdependence

<u>Archetypes</u>　　　<u>Tasks</u>

Ruler　　　　　　　generativity
Sage　　　　　　　integrity
Magician
Fool

This procedure will be covered in more detail in a later chapter.

Conclusion

This is a book about therapy, not theory. Although much of the theory on which the context of the hero's journey is based is derived from a combination of Jungian theory, post-Jungian theory and developmental psychology, the therapeutic techniques I will talk about are borrowed from many schools. My integration and combination of these therapies will probably offend therapeutic purists from each of those schools. The approach proposed in this book, however, is based on the premise that *everyone's life matters.* No matter how a problem developed, whether it be trauma, or poor parenting, bad genes, or an inability to listen to the calls of the gods, unless severe and continuing early trauma or biological distress occurred very early in life (and often even then), there is a way for each person to approach a problem, to claim his or her own life, and to find a role in the world. And, by this I do not mean adjustment to the norm (although there may be times when even that is necessary).

The preceding material is presented as a background for the therapist, not the client. It isn't necessary to teach clients that they are heroes on a journey; only to treat clients as heroes on a journey. Using the hero's journey as a context for the process of psychotherapy provides a heuristic device or a meta-theory on which we can build a practice of a client-centered therapy and transform the role of the therapist into one that is part psychologist, part parent, part healer, part mentor, part teacher, part philosopher, but most of all, a guide: one who enables others to find their own paths and solve their own problems without us. Now that we have surveyed the territory, in the rest of the book we will learn how to make this transformation. We begin with the first responsibility of the guide: finding yourself.

Recommended Reading:

Carol S. Pearson (1991) *Awakening the Heroes Within: Twelve Archetypes that Help us Claim our Lives and Transform our World*. San Francisco: Harper/Collins, the basic reference book for this work, details the stages of the journey and the levels of each of the archetypes.

Joseph Campbell's (1968) classic, *The Hero With a Thousand Faces*. Princeton, NJ: Bollingen Series, shows how the myth of the hero's journey has appeared in the myths of many cultures throughout time.

Erik H. Erikson (1963) *Childhood and Society*. New York: W.W. Norton and Company, is another classic that elaborates Erikson's concept of psychosocial stages and contrasts these with Freud's concept of psychosexual stages.

Anthony Stevens (1982) *Archetypes: A Natural History of the Self*. New York: William Morrow and Company, Inc. integrates psychiatry, psychology, ethnology and biology to present an evolutionary basis for archetypes.

Anthony Storr (1973) *Jung*. London: Fontana Press, and Robin Robertson (1992) *A Beginner's Guide to Jungian Psychology*. York Beach, ME: Nicolas-Hays. Each presents clear explanations of the major aspects of Jungian theory.

CHAPTER TWO

Finding Yourself: The Therapist's Journey

I was never lost but I was a mite bewildered for three days once.

Daniel Boone

Those who wish to leave their being and their growth unchanged should not become therapists.

Sidney Jourard

Preparation for the Journey: How to have a mission without becoming a missionary

The context in which the therapy is practiced and the process of the therapy converge in the person of the therapist. Therapeutic techniques can be taught and learned independent of a world view. In fact, they usually are. But the atmosphere in the office is not the antiseptic atmosphere of the classroom, and clients seldom respond as they did in the classroom, workshop, textbook or videotape of the master therapist. The session begins and there we are, therapist and client, each burdened with the unopened baggage of our lives. One of us has to know where we are going. And, one of us has to know whose baggage needs to be inspected and whose doesn't. In short, therapists first must take their *own* journeys.

In the 19th century, well-meaning missionaries set out to do great things and often ended up doing great harm. In the name of what they believed was holy they destroyed ageless webs of community and devastated the dignity of many of those they sought to convert to their beliefs. The same can be said for some zealous followers of psychological theories. A guide has a mission but isn't a missionary. In order to take our clients on *their* journey, instead of *our* journey, we have to have a clear sense of where we are and why we are doing what we are doing and exactly what it is that we are trying to do. We must be aware of how our work relates to our lives. It is my mission to help the reader find his or her own direction, not to convert others to my theology (or theory-ology). Each of us can seek a personal direction that tells us what we must do, not what others think we should do. For that reason, our first responsibility as therapists is to take the journey to find ourselves.

In this chapter we will meet the archetypes or inner resources as described by Pearson and become more familiar with the timeless elements of the hero's journey. We will do this by taking a journey of our own; the journey to become a therapist. In preparation for discovering our own identities as therapists we will encounter each archetype, discover its relevance to the therapeutic journey and find examples of how it manifests itself in our lives.

The 4 Archetypes and Elements of the Preparation of the Therapist

> *It is the failure of our external world to meet our needs that motivates the journey in each of us to discover that we have to take responsibility for finding and for getting what we want. No one is going to give it to us.*
>
> Carol S. Pearson
> *Awakening the Heroes Within*[1]

Preparation for the journey is about survival: how we can learn to care for and protect ourselves in the world instead of seeking care from others: how we can claim our own authority instead of deferring to the authority of others. Preparation for our own professional journeys can be as rigorous and rule-bound as childhood. The hero prepares for the journey by learning to live in the world without parents. Through study and practice, we prepared to enter the world of our work without the constant oversight of teachers and supervisors, but often we became set in our ways and unaware of the need to spiral through the journey again and relearn the lessons at a deeper level. It might help us to review our own preparation for our journeys, identify our own wounds and dragons, and re-activate the four archetypes of the preparation stage; the inner resources that Pearson named the Innocent, the Orphan, the Caregiver and the Warrior. First, the Innocent.

The Innocent

The Innocent is the part of us that trusts life, ourselves, and other people. It is the part that has faith and hope, even when on the surface things look impossible.

Carol S. Pearson
Awakening the Heroes Within[2]

- Do I still have faith in the system or have I had experiences in my training that disillusioned me?

The Innocent has trust and faith and optimism. We begin training as Innocents who have high ideals and aspirations, believing that if we work hard enough and do things right we will be able to help others and make a contribution to the world. The idea of becoming a therapist is attractive to the innocent part of us who believes that other people and institutions share our ideals and motives. Often, however, the training process, or the requirements of the real world, trample the innocent trainee and the experienced therapist alike and force us to face the inevitable *fall*. How we recover from that loss of innocence will determine in large part how we treat our clients and how we regard ourselves as therapists.

The Fall

A journey can begin with a call or a fall. A fall is any situation that compels us to see things as they really are; after a fall nothing is ever the same again. Frequently clients turn to therapists for help after a fall or a great personal disappointment. Because so much of our work involves helping our clients to face their fall, we have to be especially attentive to situations in which we lose our own innocence and become cynical and un-empathic.

On professional journeys in graduate school idealistic students often face major disillusionments when they can't enroll in prerequisite courses or when they find that they aren't capable of meeting the demands of course work or internship. Others faced a fall when the rules changed in the middle of the game and managed care imposed a new reality on their clinical practices.

Emily, the Innocent

All of Emily's friends encouraged her to become a therapist. At work everyone brought their problems to her. She was always willing to listen and gave good advice. Emily looked forward to having a job where she could use these skills all the time instead of at coffee breaks and at lunch. Emily applied and was accepted into graduate training and then came the "fall." Her preliminary course work was not interesting to her and some of her professors held unreasonable expectations for the students, had poor teaching skills and used unfair grading practices. The Innocent Emily felt deceived and abandoned — Orphaned by the program that had promised her so much and delivered so little.

The Orphan

When the Orphan is dominant in our lives, the world seems a pretty hopeless place. We have been abandoned by whatever parental figure might rescue us and are left with a landscape inhabited by two kinds of people: the weak who are victims, and the strong, who either ignore or victimize the weak.

Carol S. Pearson
Awakening the Heroes Within[3]

- What are my wounds? Have I recovered? How can I access my own Orphan?

- How did I respond when I was disappointed in my teachers or my program?

- How do I Orphan myself?

Experiences of abandonment, betrayal, victimization and neglect activate the Orphan archetype in all of us. Although we all begin in a state of innocence, somewhere along the way we suffer major disappointments in our lives or in the course of our training, and it is very possible to be overtaken by the Orphan archetype and emerge as low level or shadow Orphans: cynical, mistrusting and disillusioned. When we refuse to acknowledge this part of ourselves we will have difficulty meeting it in others. When we become aware of our own Orphaned selves, or parts of ourselves, we acquire the capacity for empathy.

Our Orphan self is our most vulnerable part, but as we struggle to meet all of the requirements of rigid training programs or face the uncertainties of the job market or the drastic changes that have taken place in our profession in the past few years, *few of us can allow ourselves to acknowledge our own Orphans, our own fears and uncertainties. When we neglect or deny these feelings, we essentially abandon (orphan) ourselves.* Our training often teaches us to be objective and to ignore our own feelings and sensitivities but we have to find a way to attend to our own feelings as well as to those of our clients. When we abandon ourselves and ignore our own insecurity and weakness we lose the ability to become connected to frightened and sensitive clients. Then, we become authoritarian, rather than compassionate. We wonder why others can't handle themselves as well as we have. We begin to tell other people how they should behave.

The gift of the Orphan —the gift that we receive when we acknowledge the Orphan — is that we learn how to join together with others and receive the support of peers instead of having to seek support or acknowledgment from authority figures for the rest of our life.

> Emily needed to face the fall; the reality that graduate school was not living up to her expectations. At first she orphaned herself by directing all of her attention to others and focusing on the way that they had disappointed her. Her first response was anger that she directed at the institution and her professors and she spent many hours complaining about her fate with people who had no power to do anything about it. Later, however, she joined together with other students to complain and to protest. As a group, the students were more effective in making themselves heard than Emily could have been if she continued to act alone. She gained support in the knowledge that her complaints were justified. However, when she faced the situation realistically and realized exactly what she would have to do to become a licensed professional, she began to re-examine herself and ask if this was what she really wanted to do with her life.

Although the wound that precipitated Emily's fall was not a mortal one, there are other wounds that, unattended, can have a profound impact on the way we live and work.

Wounds

- If there was a wound that called me to this work, has that wound healed, or am I expecting the work to heal it?

Wounds are blows struck by others; the visible and emotional evidence of the fall. *They can make us stronger or cripple us for life.* A wound can be any experience that makes us aware of our own weaknesses or vulnerability. Often psychological wounds are blows struck by words that make indelible impressions on a malleable child or vulnerable adult. Abuse is a wound. Abandonment is a wound. Child sexual abuse is a wound that precipitates a premature fall from a state of innocence.

The wounded healer

Many of us were called to our work because of our own wounds: those who were sexually abused who become sexual abuse counselors, recovering alcoholics who become chemical dependency counselors, or rehabilitated gang members who return to the inner city to work with troubled youth. Once healed, traumatic experiences open avenues of awareness unavailable to those who have not experienced them. The wounded healer relates easily to the wounded client and can offer the support and acknowledgment that are vitally necessary. To have suffered many wounds gives the wounded healer powers that others cannot have.

Ultimately, however, to be of therapeutic help, the healer must herself be healed. Abuse victims who become counselors and who have not yet healed the wounds of their own abuse often become superior advocates for their abused clients, but run the risk of being poor therapists for them. In some cases these therapists so completely identify with their victimized clients that they over-protect them or fight clients' battles for them, and in so doing, keep those clients in a state of dependency. On the other hand, the therapist who has healed from her wounds does not re-live her own trauma with every client. Moreover, because she has experienced a healing process herself, she has faith in her clients' capacity to do the same and, ultimately, to learn to fight their own battles. Furthermore, the healed wounded healer is especially sensitive to the ways that therapists who have not had (and healed) similar wounds can also unwittingly re-victimize their clients.

- Doreen, an intern at a mental health agency, arrived at every supervision session outraged at the mother in the family she was seeing. "The mother is a bitch. She continually undermines the daughter. She deceived me into thinking she was willing to work on reconciliation and then spent the session reading the daughter the riot act. She doesn't want to have a good relationship with her daughter; she just wants to prove she's right. I worked hard to build up a trusting relationship with the daughter and now mom has sabotaged it all." Doreen's face is red, her voice high pitched. She prides herself on her ability to work with adolescents and feels that she has been manipulated by the mother.

Doreen became a therapist without having worked out her traumatic relationship with her own abusive mother and she continues to do battle with her every day. For Doreen, each therapeutic encounter with an unpleasant mother mirrors and evokes her own relationship with her mother. Until her wound is healed, until she develops autonomy and a self independent of her mother, she will not be able to be an effective therapist, but she could be a very effective advocate for abused adolescents.

- Terese, a victim of childhood sexual abuse, became a therapist to help others who had suffered as she had. She is a militant fighter in the just cause of exterminating sexual abuse and sexual harassment. However, as an active personal advocate for her clients she initiates confrontation sessions in which she invites the client to confront her abuser within a therapy session where Terese serves both as a mediator, a protector to her client, and a prosecutor to the accused.

> - Katherine, another victim of childhood sexual abuse, also became a therapist in order to help others. She, however, has recovered from her wounds, and although she is as fierce a fighter as Terese, and works hard for the protection of children and vulnerable adults, in her therapeutic work she enables her clients to resurrect their residual strengths and competencies. Thereafter, they re-write their own stories that change from a passive voice, that concentrates on victimization and the evils that others have inflicted on them, to an active voice that speaks of triumph over adversity.

Doreen and Terese continue to do their own unfinished therapeutic work through their clients. They have not healed their own wounds and their clients are in danger of having their lives revolve around the wounds of childhood and never choosing a path of their own. Katherine, having completed her own therapeutic work, is free to focus all of her attention on the individual needs of each of her clients and therefore able to empathize with each of them instead of identifying herself with all of them.

On the journey to become a therapist we have to explore the unexamined parts of our lives so that these parts do not interfere with our ability to do good therapeutic work. Many of us unwittingly come to this profession in order to solve our own personal problems. I've heard therapists joke that they chose to become therapists so they could be in therapy for the rest of their lives. Like most statements made jokingly, this one carries a ring of truth. However, only when we are aware of our own wounded selves can we be free not to project them on to others, or protect them from others, and only then are we capable of discriminating between our own pain and that of our clients. To help us examine our own wounds we can call on the archetype of the Orphan.

The Caregiver

The myth of the Caregiver is the story of the transformative quality of giving and even, at times, of sacrifice.
Carol S. Pearson
Awakening the Heroes Within[4]

• How do I call on my internal Caregiver and give care to myself?

The Caregiver is our capacity to love and care for each other. Without this most sublime of all the archetypes our species could not survive. The word therapy, itself, summons images of being cared for, and within the one who is providing the care it invokes the powerful Caregiver archetype who "seeks to help others and make a difference through love and sacrifice."

As therapists we will call on this part of ourselves more often than any other part. For that reason we must learn to honor and respect the Caregiver, ever mindful that on her shadow side lurks the misguided martyr who totally sacrifices self for others and in doing so helps neither. When the Caregiver is the only archetype activated therapists feel indispensable and clients quickly become too dependent. We have to remember to care for ourselves, as well as for our clients, but never to take care of ourselves at the expense of our clients, or take care of people who can care for themselves.

> **A Shadow Caregiver:**
> Carol sees herself as the ultimate Caregiver and encourages her clients to phone her any hour of the day or night. She cannot leave town without lengthy sessions with a backup therapist who must agree to be on call for 24 hours a day. Carol schedules sessions all hours of the day and often on weekends. It is not unusual for her sessions to run over-time. She looks haggard and distraught, and feels disappointed and angry with her clients and complains to her co-workers when clients don't seem to appreciate all the sacrifices she is making for them.

The Caregiver is the archetype that allows us to give care to others and to ourselves but caregiving in itself is not enough for our survival. We must also be able to protect and defend ourselves and others, and that requires the aid of the Warrior archetype to help us claim the inner authority to fight our dragons.

The Warrior

Dragons

The need to take the journey is innate in the species. If we do not risk, if we play prescribed social roles instead of taking our journeys, we feel numb; we experience a sense of alienation, a void, an emptiness inside. People who are discouraged from slaying dragons internalize the urge and slay themselves by declaring war on their fat, their selfishness, or some other attribute they think does not please.

Carol S. Pearson
The Hero Within[5]

The dragon we must slay is no more than the monster of everyday expectations about how we ought to live our lives.
                                    Sheldon Kopp

• Are there dragons that I have to fight on this journey?

The world is full of dragons: they come silently and swiftly without our awareness. We may only become aware of them when we hear interior voices saying "you should," or "you can't," or come face-to-face with the realization that we can't admit that we don't know something, or can't say, " I was wrong." David Whyte calls this "the world's fierce need to change you."[6] The professional world, too, has a fierce need to change us and make us conform. Dragons abound in each world.

Nieitzsche described the dragon as a monster covered with scales on which were written the words, "thou shalt." [7] Battles with dragons of other peoples' expectations require clever strategy; for other peoples' expectations — the world's harsh need to change us — have a way of insinuating themselves into our lives surreptitiously. What began as external pressure mysteriously takes up residence within. Soon we hear the interior voices saying, "I should," or "I can't," and begin the battle with the dragon inside ourselves, where instead of challenging the authority of others we awaken our own authority (in the language of our Warrior archetype) and say out loud, "I will," "I can," "I won't."

This is not to say that there aren't real dragons in the external world that keep us from claiming our inner resources and sharing them with the Kingdom. Sometimes we sabotage ourselves, other times we are undone by others. A mate who belittles us, a supervisor who makes unreasonable demands, or unexpected events that create unplanned for expenses that must be handled immediately, can become dragons who derail our plans and prevent us from completing the journey. Nonetheless, we can cope with both sorts of dragons by claiming our internal authority and taking responsibility for our own actions.

Today, many therapists working in changing health care settings tell tragic stories about the impossible expectations of their supervisors and administrative staff. They describe towering stacks of paper work and unreasonable demands that they see more clients in less time. Most important, they lament that clients who desperately need care often aren't receiving it. The situation these therapists describe is one we must confront in the real world in our dealings with management, insurance companies and with clients. At the same time, however, another part of the battle must be fought with our own internal dragons of dealing with authority. We fight these inner battles by embracing the inner Warrior and setting limits and goals for ourselves and embracing the inner Caregiver and taking care of ourselves and nurturing ourselves instead of expecting the work place or other institutions to do it for us.

Richard finished his course work years ago but his dissertation remains unfinished. Time is running out yet Richard continues to procrastinate. There are always "good" reasons for this, and always other areas that attract him. At the same time he has taken on more and more responsibilities in his job that prevent him from concentrating on his dissertation. Richard's dragons are internal and his decisions his alone.

Harold, on the other hand, has not completed his dissertation because his advisor continually raises the standards by asking for more measures to be included or more analyses to be run. Harold's advisor slashes away at rough

> drafts and asks for re-write after re-write. Dissertation dragons come in all shapes and sizes. Harold's time, money, and patience are running out. Harold's problem is not a psychological problem but a problem in his environment and he will need external resources and allies to solve it. In addition, however, Harold will have to activate his internal Warrior help him know when to stand up for himself and when to give in to superior forces.
>
> Alice hasn't finished her dissertation because her husband will not cooperate with child care and won't take on his share of family responsibilities. It is not Alice's choice that she hasn't finished and consequently isn't able to do the work that she loves. However, she will have to face her internal dragons (her own feelings about her relationship with her husband) and her external dragons (her husband) to come to a decision about her choices.

Dragons are persistent. We meet and conquer them again and again in our lives. The slaying of a dragon is not a one time event or milestone that once passed need never be passed again.

The Warrior Within

The Warrior within each one of us calls us to have courage, strength, and integrity; the capacity to make goals and stick to them; and the ability to fight when necessary, for ourselves and others.

Carol S. Pearson
Awakening the Heroes Within[8]

• How do I call on my Warrior to set limits in my professional life?

We and our clients need to learn to balance our lives and set limits on what we will and will not do by calling on an interior Warrior. The high level Warrior is a protector and defender, not an aggressor. The Warrior is the part of us who has high ideals and can step in and take charge when love and sacrifice aren't enough, and courage and discipline are needed to make difficult decisions or to stand up for ourselves against institutions and others who threaten the well being of our clients and ourselves.

> ### The High Level Warrior/Caregiver Therapist
> Annette takes firm control of the length of her sessions and her appointment schedule. She is flexible enough to be available to her clients for genuine emergencies but, interestingly, these are rare. Her own sense of order and stability and willingness to set her own limits have a calming effect on her clients who know that when they are with her they have her complete attention and they are safe because she knows her own limits.

When we are operating out of only one archetype, it is as if we were blindfolded and had one arm tied behind us; we have no access to our other resources. The Caregiver and the Warrior represent the internal parents (or teachers) who enable us to survive on our own in the world and nurture and protect ourselves. Much of our therapeutic work involves helping others activate these two most powerful archetypal forces.

Once again, if we can't set limits on ourselves, as therapists, and delineate the boundary between self and other, we cannot teach others how to do this. All of these qualities and archetypes have to act in harmony with each other to help us accomplish the successful building of an ego; to help us break out of a state of dependence on others and learn to depend on ourselves.

Being a therapist is not an easy job. Not everyone respects what we do. In some quarters there is stigma attached to those who go to a therapist. Then, too, some

in other professions (and even in our own) discredit what they regard as the non-scientific nature of particular methods of psychotherapy. In preparation for the therapist's journey, we need access to:
- our Innocent in order to have faith in our ideals and beliefs,
- our Warrior to stand up to unjust criticism and to know our own limits,
- our Orphan for compassion for our clients and the ability to work together with others, and most of all,
- our Caregiver to be ever-attuned and sensitive to the needs of the client and ourselves, but also ever-aware that, within the therapy session, the needs of the clients come first.

The Preparation phase of the journey is concerned with survival and autonomy; the Soul Journey phase is concerned with meaning. In the Preparation phase we learned about autonomy, survival, literal life and death, and relationships with those who often have more power than we do.

Next, in the Soul Journey phase, we plunge into the existential, the abstract, the inner world of the imagination, the unconscious and the surreal, to find identity and the course that is ours.

True North

The 4 Archetypes and Elements of the Soul Journey of the Therapist

The soul is the dark and earthy soil where we can cultivate the higher power within us. We get to know our souls by exploring our dreams, fantasies and imagination, territories where nothing is forbidden.
Sheldon Kopp[9]
All God's Children Are Lost, But Only a Few Can
Play the Piano

The soul defies definition.
Thomas Moore
Care of the Soul[10]

When deprived of theological overtones, soul is a useful psychological term because it implies the involvement of the transcendent, the suprapersonal, the eternal, the phylogenetic. In fact, it represents the whole psychic equipment operating as a totality.
Anthony Stevens
Private Myths: Dreams and Dreaming[11]

It is said that life is not a problem to be solved but an impenetrable mystery. I believe it is both. In the Preparation for the journey, and on the Return, we face and solve the essential problems of life. On the Soul Journey we encounter the mysteries, the ambiguities and the abstractions. It is easy to talk about the soul, but difficult to decide how to encounter and care for the soul in psychotherapy. Unless we study existential or Jungian psychotherapy it is possible to complete a training program as a psychotherapist without once mentioning soul. Yet soul is our essence, and once we have awakened the archetypes of the ego, and identified our wounds and dragons, we are ready to turn inward and experience its complexities.

The concept of soul is slippery and elusive. Thomas Moore claims that the soul defies description and has to be experienced. David Whyte says, "Soul is measured by vitality, by depth of feeling, and by depth of thought. But most of all it is measured by the experience of participation."[12] We can now experience the archetypes of the soul by asking ourselves some very simple questions; questions whose complicated answers come, not from the head, but from the heart. These questions are: What do I seek? What do I love? What do I need to create? and What do I need to destroy?

The Call
• What was my call to this work?

The true vocation of the human being is to will to be oneself.

Irvin Yalom

The word "vocation" is derived from the Latin *vocare,* meaning "call," and is defined as a divine call to, or a sense of one's fitness for, a certain career or occupation.[13] Joseph Campbell described a call as the signal that heralds the need to begin the journey. He wrote, "... no matter what the stage or grade of life, the call rings up the curtain. The familiar life horizon has been outgrown; the old concepts, ideals, and emotional patterns no longer fit; the time for the passing of a threshold is at hand."[14]

Most of us, however, experience neither a divine call nor a dramatic ringing up of the curtain. More than likely we hear only a whisper; we sense that something is missing in our lives; or we feel dissatisfaction with our present work. In order to be able to hear the call we have to put ourselves in situations where we can be receptive to a call. We have to learn to listen to ourselves by tuning out others and tuning in to our own desires and intentions.

❈ ❈ ❈

My Story — My Call

I was deaf to a call for many years while I attended to the practical matters of earning a living and raising a family. Like so many other women of my generation, I didn't think I had choice about a career. I was told that I could be a nurse, a teacher or a secretary and it was assumed that I would only want to hold a job until I found a husband. As I had no desire to be a nurse, none of the skills to become a secretary, and because I liked school and was interested in learning, I chose to become a teacher. But secretly I always believed that I wanted to be a lawyer and I told myself that if the opportunity ever arose, I would apply to law school.

Many years later, when I was considering graduate school options, I was surprised to find myself excited and eager to enroll in almost every course the catalogue listed under programs in psychology, and bored when faced with the thought of having to sit through courses in real estate law or torts. At that moment I realized that I'd been waiting for an opportunity to arise instead of following a call, and at last I had reached a time and place in my life when I could choose to do something because it was interesting to me because it called to me — not because it was it was practical or someone else wanted me to do it. I hadn't wanted to study law, I had simply thought that I wanted to *be* a lawyer. Now I could see that I wanted to *do* the things a psychotherapist does.

In addition to the call that summons us to a particular vocation, there is the call to a new journey when we realize that we have strayed from our own paths. The threat of change may be difficult to recognize as a call. Only gradually do we know that we are lost. I didn't recognize the call at first: I heard a new call on the day when I found myself spending more time responding to the demands of an insurance company than I had spent working with the client in question. I was being asked to reduce a complex woman to a pathological label, and to confine my treatment plan to a list of strategies and techniques designed to meet the approval of the reviewer. I realized that the incursions of managed care were leading me in a direction that I didn't want to travel. My role as a therapist was being defined by someone else. I began to doubt my professional identity and integrity.

❊ ❊ ❊

The Seeker

The quest always begins with yearning, We feel discontented, confined, alienated or empty. Often we do not even have a name for what is missing, but we long for that mysterious something.

Carol S. Pearson
Awakening the Heroes Within[15]

- What do I seek?

Seeking has to do with a search for meaning. Seeking can be a spiritual quest as well as a psychological or philosophical one. The question, "What do I seek?" is difficult to answer but the very act of asking this question can call forth the part of us that is the Seeker. And the quest begins. Uneasiness with the status quo indicates a call, and being willing to acknowledge that uneasiness (to feel one's own discomfort instead of trying to medicate it or dismiss it or rationalize it) is the beginning of a journey. Asking *"What do I seek?"* is quite a different question from asking *"What is wrong?"* (the question usually asked). To ask, "What do I seek?" pulls us inside of ourselves and demands that we listen to ourselves, for no one else can answer this question.

❊ ❊ ❊

My Story — My Seeker

Looking back, I realize that when I first became a therapist I often took my clients on my journey, instead of helping them to find their own paths. In the beginning there is a therapeutic innocence and conviction that the way one learns to "do therapy" is the right way. At first it seemed that all I had to do was nurture and protect my clients and follow the rules learned in school and in internships. The clients, however, hadn't learned the same material that I had and the techniques that once worked ultimately began to feel sterile. Something was missing: something inexplicable; was it more depth, more soul?

We spiral through the metaphorical journey repeatedly; sometimes re-learning a lesson, other times setting off in new directions. The journey that led me to write this book began on the day I knew things weren't right, and that I had to begin to search for something different. I wanted to find a way to bring soul into my practice of psychotherapy, but at that time I wasn't even sure what soul was. I was only certain that I didn't like the way I was being forced to think about my clients. Awareness of a call to a journey was especially unwelcome at my stage of life when I thought I had arrived at a destination. I believed I'd reached the end of my career and could look forward to retirement. Yet, I felt uneasy. Things that once seemed certain to me no longer were, and I had a sense that I had lost my way. I set off on a quest, uncertain of a destination.

❉ ❉ ❉

The Lover

Without love, the Soul does not engage itself with life
Carol S. Pearson
Awakening the Heroes Within[16]

- What do I really love and feel deeply about?

Anyone who has ever fallen in love knows how difficult it is to define love and how powerful and totally unreasonable this archetypal force can be. We need all of the strength of the inner Caregiver and Warrior (the primary archetypes of the ego) to keep us from making foolish choices or doing things we might later regret. However, there is more to love than romantic love and there are many different kinds of passion. For that reason we must allow ourselves to know *what* we love in addition to *whom* we love.

Most traditional programs in psychology seldom speak about love or passion except as it relates to sex. Love, however, is the strongest power on earth and is essential to our survival. What we love makes visible our essence and allows others to see who we are. Through love we experience the soul.

Awakening the Lover archetype (discovering what it is that we love and feel passionate about) enables us to follow our bliss because the Lover knows what our bliss is. However, "bliss" involves more than pleasure and exhilaration, and following our bliss or making a commitment calls for work and discipline — strange bedfellows for the soul.

❋ ❋ ❋

My Story — My Lover

I must confess that I had never really understood what people meant when they asked to be loved for who they are. Then, I read a line in a poem by David Whyte called *This Time:*

> " The stars told him
> they loved him loved him only
> for what *he* loved himself.
> they did not love him
> for what he was."[17]

and it was clear. I realized that I might love infants and small children simply for being who they are, but I love others for those things they are passionate about.
Now I had to become aware of what I loved and to let myself know what my desires were. I had to examine my own soul instead of figuring out what others wanted and thought I should want.

I embraced the Lover archetype, in this case, and followed my "bliss" by reading, studying and training with teachers I admired. I found my way into the world of poetry, myth and fable, searching all the while for ways to bring these elements into my work in ways that were responsible and respectful to my clients.

❋ ❋ ❋

The Creator

Creativity is the ground of any well-lived life. We all create our lives by the choices that are available to us about the ways we live them no matter how circumscribed those choices might be.

Carol S. Pearson
Awakening the Heroes Within[18]

• What do I long to create for myself personally and professionally?

The Creator archetype comes into our professional lives when we create our professional selves by claiming what we love and making it an important part of our lives. To do this requires using the soul's greatest tool: the imagination. Robert Johnson calls the imagination the "image forming capacity in the mind, the organ that has the power to clothe the beings of the inner world in imagery so that we can see them."[19] The novelist Vladimir Nabokov described the imagination as the "muscle of the soul." The Creator flexes this soul muscle and brings ideas and images into our consciousness that allow us to re-create ourselves and our worlds.

Using the imagination allows us to envision what it is that we want for ourselves and thereby enables us to find a way to obtain our goals. Robert Fritz claims that we can't create until we have a vision of what we want to create. Otherwise, he argues, we follow the path of least resistance and continue to do things as we have always done them. The path of least resistance soon becomes a rut.[20] Creating a vision, and following that vision, changes the underlying path, but acting on that vision requires an exertion of the muscle of the imagination (and every other muscle we have).

Like any muscle, the imagination needs constant flexing or it becomes useless. By envisioning and naming what we want —saying it out loud, or writing it down — we bring something new into existence and make it more difficult for ourselves to settle for lesser goals. We begin to participate in life instead of being mere spectators. Again, because *we* have participated in life, we know that it is possible for our clients to participate as well.

❊ ❊ ❊

My Story— My Creator

My vision came together slowly. I imagined that I wanted to write a book to use as a text for a course for beginning therapists, but that was a faint trace of the outline of what was to come. However, it was a beginning; an idea or vision that hadn't been there before. Creating the vision is only a first step but without it we might wander aimlessly or be like those who wait all their lives to hear the call

As my vision unfolded I soon found ways to bring poetry, drawing and dreams into the therapy session, and when I did, I found that my clients opened doors into their inner lives that in many cases allowed them to find their own passions and to give voice to their own desires.

❊ ❊ ❊

The Destroyer

Whether we believe in an afterlife or not, until we stop denying the reality of death, it will inevitably possess us.

Carol S. Pearson
Awakening the Heroes Within[21]

- What outmoded or borrowed ideas or dreams do I need to let go of?

Claiming one's own life is liberating, but requires letting go of old resentments, of outmoded beliefs, and of the idea that we can know it all or do all things perfectly. Forgiving and letting go are two of the most difficult endeavors we face, but they are also the most liberating. To forgive and let go frees us from carrying other people's baggage on our journeys. Holding on to the heart's desires is not the same thing as hanging on to childish dreams. The Destroyer helps us to let go of impossible dreams and make room for the possible.

Creating and destroying go hand in hand. The Destroyer archetype enables us to give up and let go of all the things that we don't need on our journeys. This means admitting that we and our clients are mortals; acknowledging that all of our lives have endings; and realizing that neither life nor therapy is endless. The Destroyer allows us to cut our losses and to leave people and situations that aren't good for us. The Destroyer also helps us to say goodbye to our clients when they are safely started on their own paths.

❉ ❉ ❉

My Story — My Destroyer

The Destroyer helps me to know, too, that therapy isn't all sweetness and light, positive thinking, and unconditional positive regard. Understanding the Destroyer keeps me aware of the deep incomprehensible forces, inherent in all of us (forces Rollo May calls "daimons") that, when ignored, can overwhelm both therapist and client. When I am brave enough to call on it, the Destroyer lets me know rage, hatred, passion, and anger and allows me to encounter these forces in myself and my clients. (The Destroyer also helps me cut out pages of material that aren't essential to this book.)

I had to be willing to allow my clients to be angry with me. To respect their anger and not imply that it wasn't all right for them to have it. There are relationships that must be broken and there are times that therapy must end. I had to let go of my suppositions there was one right way to do therapy. I had to clean out my own theoretical closet and get rid of the things that were no longer useful: to open my mind and forget my own ego needs of comparing myself to others.

❉ ❉ ❉

The soul archetypes are vibrant and active; powerful forces that are more easily felt than personified. When we allow ourselves to delve into the passions of the soul we become alive. Awakening the archetypes of the soul is more a matter of opening up to possibility, experiencing intense feelings and discovering what is meaningful to us: we discover who we are, we find the treasures that were always there but hidden from our view.

Treasures
- What is my treasure? What special aptitudes and talents do I have?

Our treasures are the gifts we uncover on the journey and subsequently share with the world. Treasures are things we do well, things we love, the things we unearthed in the "gentle conversations" we held with ourselves when we listened for the call. Just as we need to "tune in" to hear a call, we have to "look in" to find the treasure. Looking in begins the soul journey but once we have taken this part of the journey it is time to move on to the Return; to return to the kingdom and share our gifts with others.

❄ ❄ ❄

My Story
When I discovered Pearson's work on the hero's journey, I found a way to activate the abilities inherent in each client that enable each to find a true path. In the past I tried to be the expert, the strategist, the analyst, when most of my clients were in need of someone else, an *elder,* a guide who could point the way and enable them to continue by themselves. As a guide, I could look to the clients, the story of their lives, and the stages of their journeys, to choose and use a particular theoretical approach to help each one find the right path.

The 4 Archetypes of the Therapist's Return

It isn't over until it's over.
Yogi Berra

...helping professions must address issues that link our individual lives and our collective responsibilities. In other words, personal change lies at the heart of collective change, and the interactions between individuals and their worlds are complexly reciprocal. Changes in either will trigger changes in the other, even when the persons involved are relatively unaware of or apparently uninterested in the larger spheres they influence."
Michael J. Mahony, *Human Change Process*[22]

All hero myths emphasize the importance of the return, but only recently have therapists begun to recognize the importance of social responsibility.

At journey's end the hero returns to the community to share the treasures. At the end of the therapist's journey we achieve clarity about our own missions and respect for the missions of others. Here we combine all of the resources we acquired in the preparation and soul phases of our journeys. We mark the boundaries of our kingdoms, do our work, continue to learn and pass on what we have learned to others, and, last but not least, enjoy!

The Ruler

The Ruler as an archetype is about claiming your own power for good and for ill.

Carol S. Pearson
Awakening the Heroes Within[23]

The Ruler is the combination of the Warrior and the Caregiver. When we combine these two archetypes we are able to take on the task of responsibility for others outside of ourselves and for ourselves in the world at large. Each therapist must ask: what is my kingdom? For whom and for what am I responsible?

- What is my responsibility to others? Who is responsible for the outcome of therapy? What kinds of problems am I willing to consider as legitimate therapeutic concerns?

Family therapist and psychiatrist Carl Whitaker told his patients, "I will take charge of the therapy and you take charge of your life." When therapists try to take charge of clients' lives we prevent their departure on their own journeys. However, we, not the client, are in charge of determining the boundaries between therapy and life. In listing our competencies we stake out territories and say, "These are the things that training and practice have prepared me to do. Although I can't guarantee the desired outcome every time, I will be responsible to safeguard my client and to take responsibility for the therapeutic encounter."

❄ ❄ ❄

My Story — My Ruler

I believe that in one sense I am responsible for the outcome of the therapy. If therapy is not succeeding it is up to me to terminate the therapy and suggest another therapist, and to do this in such a way that I don't make a client feel untreatable. I am responsible to give each client my full attention, to continue to study and learn, and to make decisions that are in the best interest of the client. In this regard I try to emulate the therapist I described in the Warrior section and I continue to seek therapy supervision.

The realization that others were defining me as a therapist forced me to think about the extent of my kingdom and to ask myself what my responsibilities are to my clients. Am I willing to be a provider for a company that allots the number of a client's sessions based on inflexible and arbitrary guidelines derived from questionable research methodology or cost saving, rather than concern for the best interests of the client? Am I willing to accept the fact that in many cases the client is no longer the client, that the third party payer is the client? Am I willing to give a client a diagnosis that may stigmatize and prevent future care? Am I willing to make my clients advocate for themselves, when they are least able to do so? Or, do I become their advocate and in so doing change the nature of our therapeutic relationship? I do not have the answers to all of these questions but I must keep asking them.

- What are the boundaries of my kingdom?

I hold myself responsible for the more mundane parts of the kingdom such as keeping records, keeping my licenses up to date, joining professional organizations, paying the bills and taxes, and making decisions about office space and allocation of resources. I don't enjoy doing these things, but they, too, are my responsibilities.

Sometimes, however, I am tempted to overstep my therapeutic boundaries and give financial help to clients or obtain special social services for them. Each of these cases requires individual consideration and must be taken to supervision (where I am usually, but not always, reminded that I am overstepping my own boundaries).

❄ ❄ ❄

The Sage

Sages have little or no need to control the world; they just want to understand it. The discipline of the sage is to cultivate a desire for truth strong enough to counter the Ego's need to be proven right.

Carol S. Pearson
Awakening the Heroes Within[24]

• What more do I need to know?

Being smart is knowing what we don't know as well as what we do and having the intellectual fortitude to keep asking questions even when that makes us feel stupid. But most of all, being a smart therapist today means avoiding the pose of the all-knowing teacher and remaining a student for life.
Richard Simon, in *Family Therapy Networker*[25]

When we awaken the Sage archetype we develop detachment and the *observing self* so necessary to maturity, to meditation, and to the capacity to observe self and other at the same time — an essential element in the therapeutic process. The Sage seeks wisdom as opposed to vindication and is the part of us that helps to keep an open mind. The Sage sees the big picture. Angeles Arrien captured the concept of the Sage when she stated that what is necessary for all of us is to: *Show up, pay attention, tell the truth, and don't be attached to the results.*[26]

❋ ❋ ❋

My Story — My Sage

There will always be more to learn and life's mysteries will continue to elude me. I have a difficult time not being attached to the results of psychotherapy. I become aware of this during a therapy session when I feel myself trying too hard to make something happen. At times like this I have to let go and remember that it is the client who is on the journey.

Continuing education concerns more than accumulating C.E.U.'s to satisfy a licensing board. It means opening up to curiosity about the world around us. Pearson conceptualizes the Sage as the archetype that results when the Lover and the Seeker join forces. Here, once again we follow our bliss with the realization that we are on a life-long quest for learning and that the greatest master is not the one who has all the answers, but the one who can pose the most interesting questions.

I learned on my journey that I do not subscribe to the medicalization of psychotherapy. Not all of my clients can or should be given a medical diagnosis. Concerns of the soul are not always *mental disorders or diseases,* but they are serious and worthy of our time, our deepest consideration, and careful and continuous study.

❋ ❋ ❋

The Magician

The power of the Magician is the power to change consciousness. Without the Magician, the kingdom cannot be transformed.

Carol S. Pearson
Awakening the Heroes Within[27]

• What do I need to change?

The journey of the therapist is above all the journey of the Magician: the combination of the powerful archetypes of the Creator and the Destroyer. Changing consciousness and awareness — awakening — is what we do, and we must do it within ourselves as well as in our clients. The power to name can be magic and, when used with care, carries with it a transformative force. Rollo May said, "Naming the problem is tantamount to the therapist's saying, 'Your problem can be known, it has causes; you can stand outside and look at it.'" [28]

The manner in which we name can itself create change. Family therapy, the brief therapies, solution oriented therapies and narrative therapy all re-named the problems of psychodynamic and analytic therapies with amazing magical results. On the other hand, the power to name has a negative side when we use it to substitute naming for changing. Making diagnoses, using labels and talking about symptoms instead of doing therapy is naming, not changing, and can be harmful when it takes away the client's power to participate in changing himself.[29] When we impose names on people we can limit them.

As therapists we have the power to change the way that we practice our craft. If we believe that change is possible we can help others make the changes they need to make. Psychotherapy is about the change process. Michael Mahony in *Human Change Process,* says, "We are participant observers in an era of dramatic change in human experience. Increasing numbers of individuals are reporting fundamentally novel ways of knowing and experiencing their lives, their selves, and their relationships to other people and our shared planet."*[30]*

❊ ❊ ❊

My Story

I believe that all of us can change something. However, I must admit that the clients who come to see me in my private practice are much more open to change than the disturbed school children assigned to me, or convicted felons ordered to treatment by the courts. However, people don't have to *want* to change to benefit from treatment or therapy. Sometimes therapists are the ones who have to change and the Magician archetype is the one we can call on to help us.

There are those who believe that change happens whenever the Magician is true to herself. This is true of therapists and clients alike. When the therapist has found her own voice (and knows her own truth) she can then empower others to do the same. I've never liked the word "empower," but no other word expresses what happens when we have fought the dragons and find our own voices. When this happens, our defenses crumble, and when we have no need for our own defenses we can learn to be fully present with our clients. In that atmosphere, magic happens.

❊ ❊ ❊

The Jester/ Fool

Fools [Jesters] have a license to say what other people would be hanged for, to puncture the Ruler's ego when the Ruler is in danger of hubris, and to generally provide balance to the kingdom by breaking the rules and thereby allowing an outlet for forbidden insights, behaviors, and feelings.

Carol S. Pearson
Awakening the Heroes Within[31]

- What needs to be enjoyed? Where is the joy and happiness in my work?

The goal of the Jester/Fool is enjoyment and pleasure, but the Jester is also the one who can tell it like it is; the child in the old story who was the only one to notice that the emperor is naked. The Jester, who allows us not to take ourselves too seriously, is cleverly demonstrated in O'Hanlon's *Six Step Recovery Program for Adult Children of Dysfunctional Theories:*

O'Hanlon's Six Step Recovery Program for Adult Children of Dysfunctional Theories:

STEP 1. We admit that we are powerful enough to create the idea of pathology in those we work and interact with. We resolve to stop imposing our beliefs on others. We will give up our theories to a lower power.

STEP 2. We vow to really listen to and acknowledge the feelings and points of view of the people we work with without closing down the possibilities for change for them in the future.

STEP 3. We resolve to treat each person as an individual, and tailor our treatment to individual needs, perceptions and goals.

STEP 4. We resolve to confront and break through our denial about people's strengths, abilities and health. We recognize that not everything people say and do has a pathological motive. We have decided not to label others in a way that disqualifies, invalidates or discourages them. We will studiously avoid hardening of the categories.

STEP 5. We recognize that humor helps break the cycle of hopelessness. People are grim enough as it is without therapy adding more to their sense of grimness. We vow to be sincere but never serious.

STEP 6. We are committed to bringing ourselves into the therapy encounter, rather than remaining distant professionals doing techniques and methods on our patients. [32]

❄ ❄ ❄

My Story — My Jester/Fool

All of us love to laugh and laughter can be healing, as Norman Cousins proved when he treated a serious medical ailment with a steady diet of old comedy films. Laughter has a place in therapy but never at the expense of anyone else. Four year old Eric and his cousins were taking their first ski lesson. When Eric took a fall and came up covered with snow, all his cousins laughed at him. Eric burst into tears. As his father brushed him off he tried to reassure him by telling him that they were laughing *with* him, not *at* him. "Dad," he sobbed, "I am not laughing." I have learned never to laugh with a client when the client isn't laughing.

However, the client and the therapist who can laugh at themselves are well on the way to mental health. I keep the six step recovery program in mind, and I admire and am amused at the same time by the power of the message of the Fool who can say in six steps so much of what I mean to convey in this book. Finally, I recall the message of the great psychologist, Ziggy, who said, *Never get too personally involved with your own life.*[33]

❄ ❄ ❄

Conclusion

Finding ourselves is a life-long endeavor for therapist and client alike. It's easy to get off course. However, now that we have examined our own journeys, and found ourselves, we are in a better position to turn to our clients and see how this model can enable us to help them find direction in a rapidly changing world.

Recommended Reading:

Pearson, Carol S. (1991) *Awakening the Heroes Within: Twelve Archetypes to Help Us Find Ourselves and Transform Our World*. San Francisco: Harper Collins, provides a complete description of the levels of all twelve archetypes, identifies the task each accomplishes and the gift it brings. Pearson describes the stages of the hero's journey and relates the archetypes to life stages, psychological type, the enneagram, and gender. *Awakening the Heroes Within* is the essential reference book for therapists who follow the hero's journey model.

Joseph Campbell with Bill Moyers (1988) *The Power of Myth*. New York: Doubleday, lucidly describes and beautifully illustrates the myth of the hero's journey.

Sheldon Kopp (1991) *All God's Children are Lost, But Only a Few Can Play the Piano: Finding a Life That is Truly Your Own*. New York: Prentice Hall Press, is a moving and powerful guide to finding your own life written by a master therapist who is also a master story-teller.

David Whyte (1994) *The Heart Aroused: Poetry and the Presentation of the Soul in Corporate America*. New York: Doubleday is an extraordinary example of the work of the Soul in the world.

Mary Oliver (1986) *Dreamwork*. New York: The Atlantic Monthly Press is a book of poetry that will change your life.

Questions to Lead You on a Self-Guided Journey

Taking a Therapist's Journey

It would seem that a logical first step in the therapist's journey would be that of being a client. While it is difficult to imagine becoming a therapist without that experience, aside from psychoanalytic and Jungian training institutions, few programs require students to participate in psychotherapy and some institutions go so far as to regard such a requirement as an invasion of the student's privacy.

On the other hand, requiring students to be clients can serve as a thorough indoctrination into the particular school of therapy practiced by the school in which they trained and, as Hillman suggests, convert students to a psychological theology.[1] The converts then identify with only one therapeutic role: (caregiver, teacher, healer, spiritual advisor, expert or warm human being); they adhere to one set of therapeutic techniques, and consider clients and therapeutic methods only as they relate to that role. In this way many of us unwittingly become "missionaries," believing that we have found the path: proselytizing to clients and colleagues alike.

The following series of exercises are designed to enable you to take a self guided journey and become more familiar with the archetypes and the elements and the stages of the hero's journey as they relate to your own life and work. The questions should be answered *in writing*. There are no correct answers to these questions, nor are the answers of any particular interest to anyone but you. Once written, they become a personal map of your professional journey and can serve as a way to reorient yourself if you get lost.

ELEMENTS OF THE JOURNEY: THE CALL

To find out whether or not you've heard a *call*, ask yourself the next few questions. Hold a gentle conversation with yourself, but answer the questions in writing. Remember, gentle conversations are also honest conversations. The point to being gentle is that you do not judge yourself, no matter how surprising your answers may be.

- *Why am I doing this (doing this job, taking this course, attending this workshop, reading this book)?*

- *What intrigues me and arouses my curiosity about this work?*

- *What personal satisfaction do I get out of doing this work?*

Maybe you want to help people and have always felt drawn to careers in which you could be of service to others. Perhaps you are intrigued by intellectual challenge and search for answers to philosophical and psychological questions about why people behave as they do. Maybe you seek meaning and purpose in your life. Or, possibly psychotherapy just seems like a good way to earn a living, or you found a graduate program that would accept you, or one you could afford. Ask yourself what keeps you going and involved in your job, your course work and your reading. If you are having trouble answering this question, put it aside and come back to it later. If you continue to have difficulty answering it, make a note of that.

ELEMENTS OF THE JOURNEY: WOUNDS

- *If there was a wound that called me to this work, has that wound healed, or am I expecting the work to heal it? What have I done to participate in the healing of my wounds?*

Even though wounds are inflicted by others, we have the power to heal ourselves. Healing wounds is an active endeavor that requires self care and self protection. What actions might I take and what thoughts might I muster, to help myself heal a wound?

If you do not have personal awareness of wounding, read the examples in the text of the wounded healer and comment on them. What is the wound? Has the wound healed? How does it affect the therapist's work and what impact might it have on her clients?

ELEMENTS OF THE JOURNEY: DRAGONS

- *What dragons must I continue to fight?*

- *What should's and can'ts do I carry around and how do they limit me?*

- *What are the expectations of other people in my family, my work place and my profession that are not congruent with my personal expectations?*

- *What am I going to do about this? What are some of the things that I can do when others have expectations different from mine?*

- *What are the barriers (both internal and external) to my growth and the awakening of all of my potential?*

Our internal barriers can be the shadow parts of ourselves that we don't allow into our awareness: the parts of ourselves that we can't admit to (good or bad). To help yourself answer this question think of people who drive you crazy, whom you can't stand, and ask what it is about them that you most dislike. This could be a shadow part that you have denied and projected on to others. Think, too, of people you most admire and look up to and wish you could emulate. Which of their qualities do you most admire? These could be other parts of your being that you haven't allowed into your awareness. Not acknowledging our own quirks and qualities can be invisible roadblocks on the journey. It is trite but true that the more you know and accept yourself the better you will be able to accept others.

- *What are my prejudices and strong beliefs that might interfere with my acceptance of my clients?*

Most of us are prejudiced in one way or another. Of course we believe that our prejudices are the "right" ones to have. We think of ourselves as fair minded, open, kind, generous and loving. But aren't there certain people who irritate you? How do you work with people who don't share your views or are openly opposed to your beliefs about politics, men's and women's issues, religion, spirituality, and sexuality?

Are there certain cultures or populations that you are unprepared to work with because of a lack of knowledge or information or because of a dislike of that particular group? I'm not suggesting that you have to like and be willing to work with everyone, only that you be aware of your prejudices as well as your competencies. Are you willing to ccontinue to let your clients teach you how to work with them?

THE 4 ARCHETYPES OF THE THERAPIST'S PREPARATION

- **The Innocent**

    Have I had experiences in my training or my clinical experience where my Innocent was disillusioned? Or is my innocent faith still intact? Where is my Innocent active in my life?

- **The Orphan**

    What experiences have I had of being Orphaned; of being betrayed by the system, or a school or an authority figure of some kind? How do I Orphan myself?

    Orphaning the self occurs when we abandon ourselves and concentrate on what others are saying and doing to us. Some who were victimized at an early age have to be taught to be aware of their own feelings because they are continually attuned to how others are feeling and live in a state of hyper-alertness.

    If you have had no experience of being Orphaned, comment on Emily's case. What would you do if you were Emily?

- **The Caregiver**

    How did I call on my Caregiver when others disappointed me, or rejected me or abandoned me?

    The ability to self-soothe is an essential survival skill. Soothing the self is not simply a matter of telling yourself that everything is all right, but of reassuring yourself that your feelings are important and worth consideration and that you can access help from your environment if that is necessary.

Here I ask you to think of ways you can talk to yourself when things go wrong. It may help to imagine calling on a *strong parental figure within who will not desert you*. Think of a situation that you might handle differently now that you are aware that you have an internal Caregiver who is always present.

- **The Warrior**

How have I made use of my Warrior to set goals, determine my limits and protect and defend myself?

When we think of the Warrior as a protector, an achiever and a goal and limit setter, we usually find that we can call on this part very easily when we are asked to help others. It may then help to imagine how you would do these things for another and then substitute yourself.

How do I make use of my Warrior and my Caregiver in my relationship to my clients?

THE 4 ARCHETYPES OF THE THERAPIST'S SOUL JOURNEY

- **The Lover**
  What do I love?

What are your passions? List all of them whether or not they seem to have anything to do with therapy. Then ask yourself what are the things you really love to do. When are you most fulfilled? What part of your life or work makes you feel most alive? What activities absorb you so much that time stands still when you are doing them? What moves you and inspires you and evokes your passions?

What awakens your Lover archetype? Are you passionate about ideals and ideas, liberty, justice, rights, and fairness? Who are the people in your life that you feel passionate about? Do you have a passion for art, music, painting, decorative arts or homemaking arts, athletic activities, politics — anything?

If there are no sparks or passions in your life, what do you propose doing about that? Do you see this as a problem?

- **The Seeker**
  What do I seek?

What are you looking for in your career and your life? Do you seek security or do you seek excitement? Are you looking for new knowledge and information? Are you looking for a different social setting? What are the situations in your life that make you feel restless and uneasy? Where is your discontent? What do you want?

The most difficult question for many people to answer is, "What do you want?" I've seen many women burst into tears on hearing that question because they realize that they have never before been asked to consider what it is that they want, only what other people want. Often they feel guilty even considering the question. Here, I am merely giving you permission to know that there might be something that you want that is different from what you have.

Give voice to the uneasiness, even if you can't answer the question.

- **The Creator**
What do I want to create for myself professionally?

Let your imagination run wild. Bringing what you want into your awareness helps you prevent unconscious sabotage. If you want to achieve success and recognition in your field, admit this to yourself at the outset. If you want to be a leader, acknowledge it. If you want to build a private practice (even in today's climate) let yourself know that is what you want. If you want to be an administrator or run a clinic, create a new school of psychology, use creative materials, art, music, movement in your therapy, give form to your creations.

It may even be that your creative urges have nothing to do with your work. Give voice to them nevertheless. Forget any practical reasons why you should not be able to create what you want. Envision yourself bringing forth your creation.

- **The Destroyer**
What do I need to destroy or let go of?

When we neglect the Destroyer, it can engulf us. Are

there instances where you are overly critical of others who don't share your views? Do you make sarcastic and cutting comments about others? Are there self destructive measures you engage in? Are you willing to acknowledge the destructive forces in yourself and your clients? Are there ways of doing your work that no longer fit and need to be discarded?

Are there people in your life who need to be forgiven and no longer carried as resentments and burdens on your journey? By this, I do not mean excused and exonerated for what they have done but that you might be free of carrying the corrosive anger that harms you and doesn't affect them in the least.

THE 4 ARCHETYPES OF THE THERAPIST'S RETURN

• The Ruler

What is my responsibility to others? Who is responsible for the outcome of therapy?

What are my responsibilities as a therapist and what are the client's responsibilities?

What are you willing to share with the community? In addition to your personal and professional kingdom, what do you owe to your larger community and to society? Are you involved in or interested in teaching, professional organizations, volunteer counseling, or writing letters to the editor, or other activities?

Do you believe that therapists have a moral responsibility to society or that the personal well being of the individual is the only therapeutic concern? Do you engage in any type of activity outside of your profession or your family that contributes to the well-being of the community or the world?

What kind of problems am I willing to consider? What are the boundaries of my kingdom at work?

What kinds of clients and what kinds of problems are you qualified and prepared to consider? What more do you need to learn in order to work with the clients and issues that interest you?

- **The Magician**
  What do I need to change?

What do you need to change in yourself, your personal life and your profession? How do you believe change happens? Can people change? How does change come about? What is the therapist's role in the change process? Surely you have heard the joke about how many psychotherapists it takes to change a light bulb. The answer is, "Only one, but the light bulb really has to want to change."

Do you think the light bulb really has to want to change? Many therapists do. Over and over I hear therapists say that they aren't making any progress because the client doesn't want to change. Listen to yourself as you think about and talk about your clients. Is it they or you who doesn't want to change? What is the therapist's role in the change process? One therapist I know calls himself a change specialist and says that his clients are experts on themselves and he is an expert on change and how to make it happen. Do you agree with that as a definition of therapy?

- **The Sage**
  What more do I need to learn?

  What areas in my field do I need to learn more about?
  What areas outside of my field do I need to learn about?

  If I could study under any teachers (living or dead) or go to any training institute, where and with whom would I study?

  Do I engage in any meditative practices to clear the mind or to get in touch with a deeper wisdom?

  Do you believe that there is any value in meditation? What do you know about it? Do you practice meditation or mindfulness in any way?

- **The Jester/Fool**
  What needs to be enjoyed? Where is the joy and the happiness in my work?

  What part of your work do you enjoy most? How might you bring more joy into your work and your life?
  Are there areas in your work where you won't allow the fool to enter? Are there places where you can not "tell it like it is?"

Finding Yourself Each Day

• **Before the session**

Even after you've found yourself you may need to reorient before each session with a different client. Take a few seconds before each session to prepare yourself for listening. Remind yourself to be alert for your own agenda and aware of your own feelings during the session.

A few minutes of breathing with eyes closed can attune you to the state of your inner world. Ask yourself: "Do I have a path I want this person to follow?" "Do I have an agenda of my own?" "Am I worried about my own performance?" "Am I willing to tolerate some silences and leave my own worries and problems behind?" Tune in to yourself and allow your concerns to come into your consciousness. Then you can put your excess baggage on the shelf until after the session.

• **During the session**

Be aware of the archetype that is awakened in you by the *words or actions* of the client. These can serve as clues to the archetype that is dominant in your client at that time. Sometimes one archetype calls out another. An Orphan may call forth a Warrior or a Caregiver. We have to find ourselves many times during the day and awareness of the archetypes that clients call forth in us helps us to help our clients.

- **Don't forget to breathe!**

  A most important aspect of therapy that is often neglected in training is attention to the breath. Shallow breathing holds in feelings, deeper breathing allows them to emerge.

  Deep breathing also enables us to center or find ourselves, to bring ourselves into the here and now. Encourage your clients to breathe and don't forget to follow your own advice.

CHAPTER THREE

Finding the Client

How to know where to begin

The first order of clinical business is to find the other, however distant, absent, or confused, who may one day tell us what he does want.

Leston Havens

Do you think you can help me when everyone else has abandoned me?

Mary

Working With Mary

Several years ago Mary appeared at my door. Her therapist had just told her he would no longer work with her. He called her intrusive, manipulative, and resistant. Mary described herself as depressed. She looked angry and said she felt abandoned and rejected. She told me she often thought of killing herself and had tried to do so several times in the past.

Mary, who was in her early thirties at the time, had first tried to kill herself when she was 16 years old and had been in therapy on and off since that time. She said she didn't remember when she hadn't been depressed. Mary claimed that her family thought she was crazy and didn't believe anything she said. They called her manipulative and said her depression and suicide attempts were merely her attempts to get attention. Several therapists had also given up on her. Mary's last therapist, who had just dismissed her

> from therapy, seemed to agree with her family. His diagnosis was Borderline Personality Disorder (DSM-IV) and his prognosis was that she was unlikely ever to change.
>
> When I met Mary she was discouraged and felt she had no options. She said if I didn't help her, she had no place else to turn. At the same time she questioned my ability to help her. She wondered if she might be *incurable,* and challenged me: "Do you think you can help me when none of the others have?"
>
> I see now that Mary was in a classic double bind; she needed me to help her but at the same time questioned my ability to do so. With many misgivings I agreed to work with her, and ultimately Mary taught me the difference between finding and diagnosing (and many other aspects of psychotherapy). I will use Mary's story to show how I learned *three essential elements of psychotherapy:* how to find the client, how to decide on a destination, and how to design therapeutic activities.

As therapist-guides, we seek to enter our clients' worlds, and stand *beside* them — not across from them or above them — in order to see the world from their vantage points and help them find their own paths. Later, it may be necessary to stand back and get a long range view of the territory in order to find a way out of a labyrinth, identify any others who may be able to help, or find those who interfere with or hinder progress. Ultimately, we have to have the flexibility and courage to change the structure of the therapeutic relationship, but before we can even stand beside them, we have to *find* them.

Many clients are lost: some don't know it. Some know where they want to go but don't know where they are. Some know where they are and not where they want to go. Some know neither. We can't know where our clients are until we *enter into their worlds and see things through their eyes.* Finding the client is the initial task of therapy and, at the same time, it is a task that never ends. In order to find clients we must develop the skills we need to discover them, to let clients know they've been found, and then to describe their present location. The skills involved in making this kind of assessment are empathic listening, acknowledgment, problem description, and listing the assets.

Finding versus Diagnosing

Many therapists have difficulty relating authentically to patients because of presuppositions and stereotypes. The training of therapists emphasizes diagnosis and classification; they are taught to objectify patients, to arrive at an APA (American Psychiatric Association) code number that pins a patient like a specimen to an admission workup or an insurance form. And, indeed, no responsible therapist can deny there is a place for diagnostic evaluation.

Irvin Yalom, *Existential Psychotherapy*[1]

A diagnosis is only a part of the finding process. Unless the client is acutely distressed and in need of emergency treatment, we should begin with a fresh perspective, and no preconceived ideas. Instead of trying to place clients or their problems into standard categories, we can find the client, and discover where he or she needs to go. A diagnosis can be a part of our assessment when that diagnosis will help clients reach their desired destinations.

Obviously we have to rule out organic illness and severe affective disorders that might benefit from pharmacological treatment,[2] but even in the course of making these determinations we must go where the client is. Although we have to gather vital statistics and information, much of this can be collected on a standard intake form because a therapist's primary task is to meet the client; as Yalom would say, *fully experiencing* the client. As guides we are less interested in where clients have been and what is wrong with them than we are in where they are now and where they want to go in the future.

An additional problem with a medical type diagnosis is that diagnoses can become indictments when they are identified as pre-existing conditions that limit insurance coverage or labels that stigmatize clients. At times, however, without a diagnosis certain clients can't obtain the therapy or the medications they need. Therefore, it is necessary to learn all we can about mental disorders and to use the standard diagnostic categories when it is in the client's best interest. But, it is not useful to *think about* clients in such limiting categories. Labels are sticky and hard to peel off. Even when we have made a diagnosis, we must continue to consider the client in the context of the hero's journey: a unique individual, a gathering of residual strengths, one who is much more than a collection of symptoms.

At first Mary lived up to all of the descriptions of previous therapists. She seemed a perfect example of the "Borderline" diagnosis and doomed to the unhappy consequential prognosis. Mary's behavior alternated between being demanding and intrusive — asking questions about my personal life, calling me at home and hanging up the phone when I answered, following me home in her car — and being withdrawn and silent — refusing to talk or look at me and staring at the floor.

For some time, I looked to the experts on Borderline Personality Disorders for advice about how to treat Mary and to determine how I should relate to her. I read all the books, talked to colleagues, and took Mary's case to supervision. I was told the protocol for working with Borderlines and tried to follow the rules. Mary and I made very little progress. Looking at Mary as a Borderline Personality Disorder I could see only her deficits. I was as hopeless as she. I found myself trying to fit her into a statistical category — the well known Procrustean bed — rather than regarding her as a unique individual, that is, an N of one. Slowly, however, I began to realize that the people who proclaimed themselves expert at treating this disorder knew a lot about "borderlines," but not very much about Mary. What was even worse, however, was that I didn't know as much about Mary as I should. I decided to forget about the experts and learn as much as I could about Mary.

I started on a different path. I remembered my training and experience in special education as a teacher of students described as emotionally disturbed and behavior disordered. Teachers didn't consider these children in diagnostic categories because a diagnosis gave us no useful information about how to help the child in the classroom. Instead, we saw each child as an individual, assessed strengths and weaknesses, and identified what each one needed to learn. Then we devised Individualized Educational Plans (IEP) based on the specific needs of each child.

Therefore, I began to look at Mary as an individual (as an N of one, a hero on a journey) and her prognosis improved. When I began to focus my attention on Mary and stopped trying to "treat" her personality disorder, she began to talk more about herself. She slowly revealed to me that she had been sexually abused by a stepfather during her early teens and when she reported the abuse her family rejected her. Seen in this light Mary's symptoms— hypervigilance, dissociation, suspicion— could be seen as the ways that she had learned to contend with untenable situations. I began to look at Mary's strengths and her coping mechanisms. After all, Mary had survived abuse and rejection by her family (and by her therapists) but had continued to seek therapeutic help through all the years. She arrived at her appointments on time and never canceled or

> missed appointments. Although she didn't have a job, she was married and seemed a good and devoted mother to her only child. I realized that I didn't need to look to the experts on personality disorders or pathology, I needed to look to Mary, learn more about her, discover how she had coped so far, and learn where she wanted to go. I didn't need to cure her or condemn her, I needed to find her.

Diagnosing and finding are, of course, not mutually exclusive. We need to do both in order to help a client find a true path. Mary's Axis II diagnosis had been a hindrance to her, especially as it labeled her with a personality disorder which can be deemed by some to be "incurable," untreatable or unchangeable. Ultimately the diagnosis of Post-Traumatic Stress Disorder was helpful and although the Axis I diagnosis of her depression eventually led to her use of helpful medication, Mary at first refused to consider medication and agreed to it only long, long after she had been "found." The chart below summarizes the difference between finding and diagnosing.

DIAGNOSING	FINDING
Limiting	Expanding
Little or no implication for change	Unlimited implications for change
Identifies liabilities	Implies Assets
Implies that the therapist is an expert	Implies more similarities than differences between therapist and client
Implies pathology	Implies possibilities

The Road to Empathy: Going Where the Client is— Empathic Listening and Acknowledgment

To find another you must enter that person's world.
                                        Leston Havens

Empathy is defined as *intellectual identification with or vicarious experiencing of the thoughts, feelings or emotions of another.* Leston Havens, whose book, *Making Contact: The Uses of Language in Psychotherapy,* should be required reading and re-reading for all psychotherapists, defines empathy as "the capacity to participate in or experience another's sensations, feelings, thoughts, or movements."[3] Havens admonishes therapists to take care not to "project your own mental state onto theirs." Whenever we project our own mental state onto clients we identify them with us and thereby lose our ability to see the world as each of us sees it. Once that happens both client and guide are lost, for we have taken away our clients' experience and turned it into ours. We have to discover clients' worlds and enter into them, not bring clients into our worlds.

Therapeutic empathy is an *active* endeavor. Entering into a client's world with no preconceived ideas takes concentration, effort, and focused attention. Havens suggests that we have to mirror clients' postures, observe their expressions, note the tone of their voices and the content of their speech, and experience their feeling states. We can even try (mentally) to complete clients' sentences in order to test our cognitive empathy. The experienced master therapist does this quickly and intuitively. The rest of us need constant practice. Fortunately, empathy is not a quality that one has or doesn't have, it is a skill that can be learned. At this point we are not looking for something that is wrong with our clients, nor are we trying to fix them in any way. As Havens says, "The goal is to comfort by our presence, not to startle by our prescience."[4] We are truly trying to understand our clients and become aware of what it is like for them to be where they are.

Empathy skills: Whole body listening: Being present with the client

The first component of empathy is listening. It is important to review listening skills each day. We've learned these skills before but even the most experienced therapist, in a rush to help, or an eagerness to have the *answer* and be perceived as helpful, sometimes rushes ahead of clients on the trail and ends up dragging clients where they want them to go instead of meeting them where they are.

There are many types of listening. We begin by noticing ourselves in ordinary conversation as we make judgments or formulate a mental reply or rebuttal while someone is speaking. This happens to the best of us when we don't keep our concentration on the task; but for now, the task is to listen. All we have to do is listen and observe with our ears and eyes and emotions. We do this by allowing the client to speak and tolerating short periods of silence while we give our total attention by:

Listening with the eyes: Focusing on expression and general demeanor.

Listening with the ears: Hearing the choice of words and tone of voice.

Listening with the body: Moving our bodies to reflect clients' gestures and posture.

Listening with the heart: Tuning in to our own feelings.

Listening with the head: Following the direction of clients' thoughts with our thoughts.

I have to remind myself over and over to listen, listen, and listen, and only then to proceed on the basis of what I've heard. My objective is to learn to work quickly without making the client feel rushed.

Finding Mary turned out to be a long and difficult process. She defined herself in terms of the restrictions placed on her in her childhood, her psychiatric diagnoses, and later in terms of her traumas. The rest of her was hard to see.

However, when at last I learned to see the world through Mary's eyes, I found a terrifying place. Mirroring Mary's physical movements and posture— shoulders slumped, head down, eyes looking up through her long bangs or down at the floor— gave me an overwhelming experience of her fear and distrust of the world. What I found when I found her was a person *frozen in time,* with no sense of a future, little enjoyment in the present; an Orphan unprepared for the journey. Many of Mary's actions and reactions were those of an ill-treated child. As she demanded more attention, I began to see that her behaviors that puzzled me were motivated by her desire to have me take care of her. Only then could I truly feel her terror and her humiliation at desperately needing to have me take care of her while being unsure of my willingness or ability to do so.

Empathy opens the door to acknowledgment. Experiencing Mary's fear made it possible for me to acknowledge that fear; something I had not been capable of when all I could see was her anger. The next step in the process was to express this to her; to let her know that she was found. This is the process of acknowledgment.

Empathy skills: Acknowledgment:
Letting them know they've been found.

The conditions of empathy are the therapist's power to imagine the experience of the other and then to express it.

Leston Havens

I recently heard a true story of a seven year old girl who told her psychiatrist that she was very, very sad. The psychiatrist looked at her sternly and said, "No you're not, you're very angry and you are using your sadness to cover it up!" If there is an opposite of empathy and acknowledgment, this is it. I think it is called distancing.

Imagine how you would feel if you were lost on a mountain top and watched the search planes passing overhead but had no way of knowing whether or not they had seen you? Or, even worse, if searchers continued to look for you on the wrong mountain because that is where they thought you should be. That's the way clients feel when we don't acknowledge their experience of being where they are or when we tell them where we think they are and our description doesn't fit their experience of themselves.

Although many clients find acknowledgment simply in our presence and attentiveness, others will know that we know how they feel only from our verbal response. An empathic response will name the client's feelings or thoughts and state the reasons for those feelings or thoughts. We must choose each word carefully because a therapist's question can open the door to the inner world of a client and we don't want to create fear or defensiveness. When we don't know how a person feels, or what they are thinking, all we have to do is ask. Again, the purpose of asking how others feel at this point is to find out where they are, not to interpret or comment on their feelings. Empathic listening and acknowledgment are essential components of therapy. These are the first steps in the establishment of trust and the foundation on which successful therapy is built.

By paraphrasing and repeating what clients say, we let them know how we've heard and understood them. When we haven't clearly understood what they wanted us to know, they can, and will, correct us. Once a client seems to feel understood it is time to move on. This procedure doesn't have to take much time but it frequently does. Some clients are very difficult to find and many therapists are too far ahead of them to be able to see them clearly (as I was when I was blinded by the Mary's Borderline diagnosis).

Now we are ready to let the client know that we have found her. She probably has some inkling if we have been mirroring her posture or breathing with her or nodding, but we want to make sure that she knows that we know where she is. The most obvious way to do this is to repeat or paraphrase several of the client's words. For example the client might say, "I've tried my best and done everything right but nothing works out for me." We might respond, "No matter how hard you try, you just can't win." By reflecting the message back to the client we show that we have heard and interpreted correctly. Remember, right now we are not trying to find out what is wrong with the client or even to suggest possibilities. We want to know what her world is like and we want her to know that she has been heard.

One type of empathic response that is useful at the beginning of therapy is a statement of the way a person feels and why they feel this way, e.g., "You're feeling down because you've put so much effort into this and haven't gotten the results you wanted." An accurate reflection identifies the client's concern and the feeling state but it is surprising how many times one hears a therapist discount the client's feelings by suggesting that they shouldn't feel the way they do.

- **Ask open and honest questions**

If you don't know how a person feels ask, "How do you feel about that?" and/or, "What do you think about that?" Don't assume that you know how someone feels or thinks because of how you might feel in that situation. Asking how someone feels or thinks is an open and honest question. It is open, in that it can't be answered yes or no, and it is honest in that you really don't know the answer. When you ask an honest question you will usually get an honest answer. Asking if someone feels angry, or hurt or defensive, may put the client on guard because there is an implication in the question that there is a certain way one should feel. This is also a closed question that can be answered yes or no and leave you at a dead end. After you find out how a client feels and what is on his or her mind, you're better able to make an empathic response. When you can't think of anything to say, say nothing. Stay connected, stay relaxed, and tolerate short silences. These elementary communication skills have to be reviewed constantly by many of us.

Acknowledging Mary

I wasted valuable time in the course of Mary's therapy before I recognized her need for more acknowledgment. An empathic response to her in the first session might have been,"You are afraid that I won't be willing or able to help you and then you'll have no place else to go."[5] Unfortunately, however, at that time I was more concerned with my own doubts and feelings than I was about Mary's. I had no idea how she felt or what was going on in her mind.

Later, when I first tried to note any signs of her accom-

> plishment or progress, Mary became even more watchful. I know now that what I had been saying did not match Mary's experience of herself and therefore she didn't believe me. I began to see that Mary interpreted my comments about what she had done well as a minimization or an ignorance of her distress and all the bad things that had happened to her. I learned to go more slowly. Mary needed her feeling state and her position to be acknowledged before I acknowledged her progress. She had to make sure that I knew how bad things were for her so that I would not abandon her. She wasn't ready to begin her journey until she was sure that she had been found. (Note: this is very different from saying that she didn't want to be found.)
>
> Mary demonstrated her unreadiness by showing her concern about what I thought and felt about her. When she asked what I wrote about her in my case notes I offered to share them with her. From that time on, at the end of each session I gave her my detailed notes and observations from the previous session. She took these home and evaluated them. She painstakingly corrected any word I used that wasn't a perfect match for her experience, and then she added her own impressions of the session and of me. In this way Mary taught me how to acknowledge her. In her writing Mary was able to say things she couldn't say to my face. Looking back over our notes she found her own evidence that she had made some change. Slowly we began to communicate; I neither labeled, criticized, diagnosed, nor praised. In this way I began to earn her trust. Mary could see that I was learning where she was, and that I appreciated how difficult it was for her to be there.

Like Mary, most clients I see for any length of time in psychotherapy are ill-prepared for the journey. Their problems are often the aftermath of abuse, violence, neglect, and family strife and as a result they may have difficulties relating to authority because they haven't developed an inner authority of their own. They also have difficulties soothing themselves or reassuring themselves. Not surprisingly, these clients are physically and emotionally dependent on others. Although many of these clients are bright, well-educated professionals who function well on many levels, in therapy, and in their primary relationships, they seem to be looking for the good parent they never had. They seek and need support and reassurance, but we have to remember that support for them is only the first step, even though that step may take a long, long time. Kind and sympathetic therapists, quite naturally, want to reassure clients that whatever happened to them as children wasn't their fault, but once we are sure that we have done that we have to move on.

Because our demonstration of warmth, concern, and support is necessary but not sufficient, once we have identified that a client is in the quicksand of victimization or dependency, our job is to get that client unstuck, not to get into the quicksand with her. The correlation of abuse, trauma and parental neglect with psychological disorders has been so well documented that it has been confused with causality and the certainty of a poor prognosis.[6] When working with dependent clients, what we, as therapists, sometimes neglect is our own experience and first hand knowledge of the resiliency of those who have been abused, neglected and traumatized. I have worked with hundreds of clients who have been abused and abandoned in every imaginable way. Their residual strengths amaze me; their ability to prevail inspired this book. When we re-frame victims and consider them heroes, who can take the same journey as everyone else, we can, and must, first acknowledge their victimization (what was done to them). But having done that we must turn their attention to what they *can do,* indeed, what they *have to do*, to continue their journeys themselves.

Empathy skills: Acknowledge with possibility

Acknowledgment with possibility is a subtle way of letting clients know that a journey is possible. When we do this we express our belief that it is possible that the client will change. O'Hanlon says, "Like Carl Rogers, we accept people where they are right now, and help them accept themselves. But then we add a little twist. We communicate, 'where you are now is a valid place to be, AND, you can change.'" For example:

Client: I fail at everything. *Therapist:* So you've failed at most of the things that you've tried.[7]

O'Hanlon adds that clients will let you know if you are *pushing the change part too hard*. This was certainly the case with Mary. Clients don't always tell us this in words. Mary became exceptionally quiet when I pushed the change part. Other clients start to argue or openly disagree. Whenever either of these things happens I know that I have temporarily lost my client and I have to find her again.

Mary taught me how to keep my eyes on my clients at all times and never to assume that I know how others feel. Luckily, not many clients are as difficult to find as Mary was and after I learned to find clients it became easier for me. However, I still lose sight of a client from time to time in a therapy session and have to backtrack to make sure that we are together.

Describing the Problem

You are here.

Before you can get where you want to go, you first have to know where you are.

Have you ever been lost in a shopping mall? The diagram that shows the layout of the mall would be useless without the x that marks the spot that shows you where you are. In the same way, when you take a journey, you need a map that shows not only where you want to go but also shows you where you are.

Many clients identify themselves as victims on the first visit. Instead of stating a problem or even identifying a symptom, they will state what they think caused the problem or the symptom. When asked why they are there they say, "I was sexually abused by my father," or "I am an adult child of an alcoholic," or "I am being abused by the people I work with who aren't being supportive of me." Or, "I would be happy if only she would..."

Be specific

Clients aren't the only ones who do this. Often when I ask a supervisee or a trainee what is troubling the client he or she will begin with a historical statement rather than a statement of the way that person is feeling or behaving in the "here and now," or what the client wants. Often I find it necessary to ask questions like, "How it that a problem to your client?" or, "Specifically, how is that now affecting your client's life?" or "Why is this person in therapy?"

If a client can't sleep, or is having flashbacks, can't make or keep friends, has periods of time when they "space out" and can't remember, or if they are hurting themselves, these are obvious signs that something is very wrong and we need to pay attention. Thankfully, however, these are things we can do something about. Yet, when a client says I was sexually abused or I'm an adult child, they are telling a part of their history or expressing the way that they see themselves. These are useful pieces of information but we need to know more. We need to learn exactly how those experiences have affected this particular individual. We've all become so accustomed to explanations and interpretations that we overlook the need to tease out, in a gentle and respectful manner, exactly how this is a problem to this client today, and ultimately to learn *how they would like things to be*.

Draw pictures

In order to clarify the situation, I often use words, geometric shapes, genograms, Venn diagrams, pictures and symbols to draw a map on a large piece of paper and put the situation in perspective and in context. When I am working with a couple or a family, or in a work situation, everyone involved can take part in drawing the map. In this way clients can begin to take an active part in charting their course.

Make sure you're speaking the same language

To my mind, in dealing with individuals, only individual understandings will do. We need a different language for every patient.

Carl Jung

If you have ever worked with troubled couples you already know how many definitions there are of the word *commitment*. It's a mistake to assume that because we speak the same language we have the same definition for abstract words. I've learned to ask clients to specify what they mean by terms like "poor communication skills," or "hard to get along with," or "unmotivated." People are not accustomed to being asked to be specific in these situations, so we have to be prepared to be patient, accepting, curious and non-judgmental.

Clients like Mary frequently describe themselves as depressed. I once assumed that I knew what they meant.

Now I ask them to spell out what they mean and I also ask how this depression is a problem in their lives. I ask clients to describe the problem or symptom in terms of how it feels, what other people notice about it, and whether any others are affected by it. I often ask clients to use "videotalk." Videotalk means to describe a desired outcome or situation in seeable, hearable, and, when possible, verifiable terms. These and other solution-oriented questions borrowed from Solution Oriented therapists Yvonne Dolan[8] and Bill O'Hanlon[9] help translate vague terms into descriptions that both therapist and client can see similarly. The descriptions form a part of the problem description and also help us see possible solutions.

Listing the Assets

Finally, an important aspect of the assessment, or the enumeration of what we do when we *find* a client, is to identify assets and liabilities. Here it is most important to focus on what clients can do instead of what they can't do or what they are doing wrong. When we find a client we identify what is there, not what isn't. This is not to say that we ignore or minimize pain, trauma, or discomfort; these are important distress signals sent up by the lost traveler. However, we have to identify the things clients can do so we can use the skills they have to acquire the additional skills they need. This is not a Pollyanna sentiment, or a type of puerile "positive thinking." A list of all the things that a person can't do, or doesn't have, would be infinite. Better to start with what they have available and what they can do, and remember what they have the potential to do. Bear in mind, if we believe, as Jung did, that there are inherent qualities and attributes built-in to the human organism, we can see why the utilization processes used by Milton

Erickson, O'Hanlon, Dolan and others are successful. When we list assets we have much more to work with than we do when we look at a disease or deficit model.

A good way to "find" clients is to look for things that we like or admire about them. We probably won't be successful in working with people in whom we can find nothing to like or admire. Sometimes, too, we can find qualities that clients didn't know they had such as persistence or loyalty or good work habits. When I was a child we received grades in something called citizenship. I was pleased to get a good grade in stick-to-itiveness. My mother, however, was amused; she had always perceived this as my stubbornness. My teacher had changed a quality others thought a deficit into an asset.

We look at our clients and ask ourselves what they have to work with. We learn a lot about the way clients talk and conduct themselves in the session. Finally, we ask about the things they've done and the ways they've coped with problems in the past and ask if there have been times when they were not depressed, or times when they accomplished a goal or solved a similar problem. If so, we can ask how they did these things.

Finding Mary

Working in these ways I found that Mary was a person who was trapped in a cage built in her past. Her diagnosis of a personality disorder had not helped her. A diagnosis of Post Traumatic Stress Disorder was more appropriate but still didn't provide a large enough context in which to see her as a hero. A diagnosis of depression was potentially helpful but Mary wasn't willing to try medication.

More helpful to me was a view of Mary as a person who looked backward on the trail, immobilized by fear, flashbacks, and intrusive thoughts. She seemed unable to ask for help and often alienated those who might help her. Mary was in need of preparation for the journey. Her hyper-vigilance and distrust of others proved that she didn't know how to protect, defend, or soothe herself. As yet she had no identity apart from her role as victim. She was a low level Orphan— living in a reactive mode.

On the other very positive hand, Mary had some good friends and a fairly supportive husband. She had a child she loved and didn't want to abandon. She was very good at taking care of children. And, she had persistence and stubbornness; all useful qualities for a successful journey. I decided to build on these.

Recommended Reading:

For additional material on empathic language and the uses of language in psychotherapy see Leston Havens (1986) *Making Contact: Uses of Language in Psychotherapy,* Cambridge, Harvard University Press, called by one reviewer, "A basic grammar of empathy—a sort of 'Strunk and White' for psychotherapists."

See also Robert Buckman, MD (1992) *Breaking Bad News : A Guide for Health Care Professionals,* Baltimore, Johns Hopkins University Press. This book contains many examples of empathic responses and a review of basic communication skills.

For examples of "possibility laced acknowledgment," see, Bill O'Hanlon and Sandy Beadle (1994) *A Field Guide to PossibilityLand: Possibility Therapy Methods.* Omaha, Nebraska : Possibility Press. This is an essential guidebook for the practicing psychotherapist and along with *Awakening the Heroes Within* is to be used in conjunction with *True North.*

Summary of Chapter Three
FOUR STEPS TOWARD THE CLIENT

The first order of clinical business is to find the other, however distant, absent, or confused, who may one day tell us what he does want.

Leston Havens

LISTEN
- Listen with your eyes: Focus on expression and general demeanor.
- Listen with your ears: Hear the choice of words and tone of voice.
- Listen with your body: Move your body to reflect gestures and posture.
- Listen with your heart: Tune in to your feelings.
- Listen with your head: Follow the direction of their thoughts with your thoughts.

ACKNOWLEDGE
- Acknowledge facts: Re-state the facts of the situation.
- Acknowledge feelings: Re-state clients descriptions of feelings.
- Acknowledge thoughts: Re-state the clients' thoughts and beliefs.
- Acknowledge possibilities: Make empathic responses that include the possibility of change.

DESCRIBE THE PROBLEM
- Use graphic language: Use seeable, hearable, feelable words.
- Use pictures and symbols.
- Define ambiguous words.

LIST THE ASSETS
- Identify previous successes.
- Identify times when the problem has not occurred.
- Identify strengths client has not previously seen as strengths.
- Identify others who can help.

CHAPTER FOUR

Deciding on a Destination: Finding Out Where the Client Wants to Go

If you don't know where you're going you're likely to end up somewhere else.

> **Mary**
> Mary: "I just don't want to feel like this all the time. I want a normal life."
> Mary had no specific goals when she came to see me and I must admit that, at first, I didn't either. She said she didn't want to be depressed all the time, and that she wanted to stop thinking about killing or hurting herself, so I focused on keeping her alive and relieving her symptoms. At first Mary was so distrustful that any attempt on my part to negotiate goals was interpreted by her as my wanting to terminate the therapy or get rid of her.

I suspect that one reason many long term therapies take so long is that neither the therapist nor the client has any idea of where they are going or any agreement to terminate therapy when they get there. It helps to begin with a sense of where the client wants to end, but this is not always easy. It isn't unusual for clients to tell us where they want to go before we, or they, discover where they are.

For that reason, this chapter could just as well come before the previous chapter. Deciding on a destination is often a part of the assessment process and like empathy and acknowledgment can also be an intervention. By discussing goals and desired outcomes we provide a structure for the therapy and reassure the client by assuming that change is possible.

The Goals of the Therapist and the Goals of the Client

It's often said that if you don't know where you're going you will end up somewhere else. That is why we need goals in therapy. The purpose of goals, therefore, is to resolve the issue or complaint of the client or make agreements to terminate therapy when some progress toward the goal has been made. We also have to differentiate between the goals of the therapist and the goals of the client.

At each step in the process of psychotherapy therapists have to find ourselves again; to examine our own philosophy and definition of psychotherapy. We ask ourselves what it is that we are trying to do and how we should go about doing it. In the goal setting process we have to separate the ultimate purpose or intent of the therapist from the immediate, more pragmatic— yes, and measurable— goals and objectives of the client.

Terms like goals and objectives offend those who contend that the purpose of psychotherapy is to make the unconscious conscious, or to re-connect clients to their essential myths and symbols, or, by working through the transference relationship, to provide the patient with an opportunity to improve his interpersonal relationships by being a person with whom the patient can interact."[1]

Statements like these, however, express the ultimate

aim of the psychotherapeutic process, or of the therapist, and can be distinguished from the more immediate objectives of the client. If my aim as a therapist is to bring clients to a realization that they have choices in life, then how, specifically, am I going to do that with this particular client at this particular time? How will my expectations match my client's aspirations and intentions? After we have asked these questions of ourselves, we ask the client; "Where do you want to go?"

Using the Guide metaphor, I think of myself as a sort of travel agent and the client as a customer who wants to take a trip but isn't exactly sure where he or she wants to go. I have to be sensitive to the kinds of things my clients like to do, what they describe as a successful trip, whom they want to take along (or who is keeping them from going), and what their resources are (are they ready to take the journey or do they need more time to gather the necessary resources). I can also be aware of possibilities that clients haven't yet thought about (trips they hadn't dreamed were possible). However, before I can suggest these trips I have first to find out about my clients and learn what they want: I have to allow them to teach me how to work with them and not assume that I am the expert who can tell others what is best for them.

Essential Techniques for Establishing Goals:
Collaborate with the client

Although some clients present themselves with specific goals in mind, most people simply want relief from pain, want a symptom to go away, or want a problem to be solved. For a client without any sense of the future, and few past experiences of success or good feelings, setting goals is a difficult endeavor. The procedure of setting goals involves respecting what clients want —

going where they are, and helping them to formulate objectives while, at the same time, continuing to make them aware of alternatives and possibilities. This delicate process is best accomplished by joining forces with the client and acting as a team. O'Hanlon describes this as "collaborative therapy" in which the "expertise of the client is given at least as much weight as the expertise of the therapist."[2]

Occasionally, in the goal setting process we learn that we and the client are not a good match. When a client wants someone else to change, wants me to be available day and night, or insists on long-term therapy at the outset, I respectfully decline to work with that client. In my solo private practice I do not have the backup I need and I choose not to be on call 24 hours a day. The sooner we learn that we are not a good match, the better it is for both of us. When that happens, however, it is essential that the *therapist take responsibility for this decision and not imply that the client is untreatable or unreasonable.*

Use magic wand and miracle questions

People are very good at telling us what they don't want and don't like, and sometimes that is all we have to go on. It isn't unusual for those who are lost (or any of the rest of us for that matter) to have difficulty deciding where they want to go or to be unaware of what they want. As I mentioned in the last chapter, clients come into my office each day defining themselves in terms of their history, or the restrictions placed on them in their early lives, or on their pathologies. These clients introduce themselves as "victims," "adult children of alcoholics," or "co-dependents." They explain their inability to act with phrases such as, "I can't do that because I was never allowed to do that in my family," or "I was punished for that or shamed for that, or told not to be selfish, so I can't consider what I want."

Such descriptions are what O'Hanlon calls problematic stories; stories that blame others for what is wrong, cite the impossibility of change, or suggest that clients have no control over their behavior. These same clients frequently believe that because it took them a long time to develop a problem or because they have felt as they do for a long time, that it will take a long time to solve a problem or cure a condition. This isn't necessarily true, but many therapists seem to share this belief and unwittingly pass it on to their clients.

Talking about goals is difficult when clients perceive themselves as helpless, or as one client called it, "deficited," or if the only thing they can tell us is what they don't want. I can simply repeat that until clients feel validated, that is, that their hopelessness or their situation is acknowledged, they will have difficulty speculating about possible goals. Problematic stories need to be challenged, but not before they are acknowledged. Once we have achieved this we can ask our clients if they want to learn how to do things differently by seeding expectancy for change.[3,4] We do this by adding a qualifying statement that implies that the situation isn't permanent. For example, "Right now it seems to you that it will take a long time for you to change."

At times like this, "magic wand" and "miracle" questions can help. These questions enable clients to picture what they want and formulate goals in behavioral or observable terms. The magic wand question is: "If I waved a magic wand and the problem went away, what would you be doing differently?" The miracle question is; "If tomorrow morning you woke up and a miracle had occurred while you were sleeping and the problem had gone away, how would you know? What would you be doing differently? What is the first little thing that you would notice? Who else would notice?"[5] By asking what the client will be doing differently, both therapist and client can identify goals and have a sense of when and how they will know that these goals have been met. Moreover, the client begins to get a sense that he or she will be able to do something different and can take an active part in the therapy. This technique is especially helpful when making a treatment plan.

Not all clients can answer the miracle question in concrete, behavioral terms. Not everyone knows what they want. We can help uncertain clients, by acknowledging how difficult this is and by being able to tolerate vagueness. O'Hanlon makes the point that the goals of therapy don't need to be emphasized immediately when the emphasis of therapy is on possibility and solution rather than on treating symptoms. However, it is always good to go back to goals when the therapist or the client feels lost. Recently, I realized that I had strayed off the track when a client asked, "Are we getting anywhere, are we making any progress?" At this point we had to stop and review what my client expected from therapy.

Are we there yet? Identify sub-goals and scale them

Parents of small children are familiar with this question which is usually asked after you have driven the first block on a fifty mile trip. The child, who isn't familiar with the scenery or is unsure of the final destination, has no way to know any of the signs along the way that tell that you are nearing the end of the trip. Clients, too, have to know how to mark progress. Without an odometer they may not even know that the trip has begun.

Asking clients to gauge the intensity of a feeling or a problem on a scale of one to ten provides a measure of progress that clients can record at various times between sessions. In that way clients will know if they are going backward or forward. When clients have vague goals, such as," I don't want to feel this depressed," I ask them to rate the level of their depression on a scale of one to ten, with ten being the worst they have ever felt and one the absence of depression. Then we have a starting point. Now we can ask what would have to be different in order for them to get to the next highest point on the scale, and then the next. In this way we develop specific criteria for each step on the scale.

It is also possible to quantify how much time clients spend "feeling depressed" and to note the times of day and activities they are engaging in that correlate with different moods. These notes can enhance the therapy and improve clients' ability to monitor and regulate their moods in between therapy sessions. In a client-centered therapy we are only comparing the client to himself or herself. Self-scaling is a way to measure internal, invisible changes.

> **Mary's goal**
>
> In Mary's case we could have quantified her depression as to the amount of time she spent feeling depressed or the intensity of her feeling or what the depression kept her from doing. Each of these could then have been related to other events or things that she was doing differently to build or impede progress. Both of us were marking her progress by different standards and it would have helped to have a shared unit of measurement.

Nonetheless, no matter how clever and skilful we may be at phrasing questions, some clients simply don't know what they would be doing differently and truly cannot answer our questions at this time. Again and again I have to re-learn to be sensitive to clients' responses because when I haven't really "found" and acknowledged my clients the very questions may sound to them as if I have no idea where they are and, consequently, no real understanding of their situation.

Negotiate solvable problems. "The person is not the problem. The problem is the problem."

There is a story told of the therapist who was asked how she would treat a Narcissistic Personality Disorder. The therapist is said to have replied, "I wouldn't let that be the problem." Solution oriented, competency-based therapists and family therapists don't have to be told to negotiate presentable or solvable problems. But many of the rest of us do. In psychotherapy, when a problem is stated as a diagnosis, such as any Axis II (personality disorder) diagnosis, or a label such as, "resistant client," "symbiotic relationship," "co-dependent," "non-motivated learner," or "uninvolved parents," the problem is not solvable because the implication is that the person is the problem or that the problem resides within the client like a genetic defect that cannot be changed. In the course of re-stating a problem possible solutions become apparent and clients are able to see that there might be an end point to therapy. This situation is similar to the problematic descriptions I mentioned before.

Sometimes all we have to do is re-define the problem. Many years ago, Bill, a farmer in his sixties, reluctantly decided to come to therapy with what he described as a "serious relationship problem." He had never before been to a therapist and sat uncomfortably on the edge of his chair with his seed cap in his hands. He said that his grown son, Arne, who lived and worked with him on his farm, was having trouble getting along with Bill's new wife, an unwanted stepmother not much older than Arne. Bill wanted to know how to help them get along together because each was refusing to give in to the demands of the other and his wife was threatening to leave if the situation didn't change. I was new as a therapist and unclear about exactly how to frame this as a psychological problem and just spoke my thoughts out loud, "So, all you have to do is decide if you want to spend the rest of your life with your son or with your wife." He stood up, handed me my hourly fee in cash and said, "Thank you very much. I know how to make that decision, I just didn't know how to get them to like each other and get along."

Therapists are also guilty of *stating problems in unsolvable terms*. I often hear therapists slipping into this mode and complaining of resistant clients, or "borderlines," or hear them label clients as passive aggressive, or listen to them blame clients for not wanting to change. Our challenge is to find a way around unsolvable situations by taking a different point of view and, at the same time, respecting our clients' innate ability to change the course of their lives. We can't assume that we know what other people's intentions are or know whether or not they want to change.

Making Mary's problem solvable

To think of Mary as a Borderline Personality Disorder was to present her as an un-solvable problem. Her PTSD (Post-Traumatic Stress Disorder) diagnosis was a bit more helpful because there was a correlation between what had been done to her and the symptoms that she had developed in her attempts to cope. However, when I extracted the problem from the person I found that Mary was a person whose problem was that she hadn't learned to take care of herself, to soothe herself, and to protect herself and to stand up for herself. This is potentially a solvable problem, especially when a therapist is able to consider a client in the context of the hero's journey, and as one who has access to the inherent inner resources we call archetypal energies. Furthermore, simply by removing the problem from the person we make it solvable. That is, it could be said that Mary was a person who "did" Borderline Personality Disorder, or PTSD not a person who "had" a personality disorder or PTSD.[6] We have to be careful, however, when speaking to clients about "doing personality disorders" or "doing depression" that we don't give them the impression that we are blaming them or implying in terms of New Age guilt that they did something to deserve this.

Ultimately, as Mary began to trust me and realized that I knew how bad things were for her, she started to believe that some change was possible. She became more willing to discuss what she would like to accomplish in therapy. Mary's usual response to any perceived threat was to become quiet and withdrawn, to hurt herself, and to think and talk of killing herself. We decided that she needed to learn to face these threats and to soothe herself, protect and defend herself so that every situation would not feel so threatening.

Mary wanted to be able to cope with intrusive thoughts and flashbacks, to stand up for herself without being aggressive, to take proper care of her body, and, finally, to set limits on her intrusive and demanding family members. She realized that an indication that she would have reached some of these goals was that she that she would be able to hang up the phone when her mother insulted her, she would begin to treat her body well by eating properly and exercising, and she would be looking directly at people instead of hanging her head. These objectives, behavioral indicators of much deeper and more intrinsic change, were things that Mary could accomplish.

Goals and objectives have to be meaningful to the client and agreed on by both client and therapist and, whenever possible, they should be explicit. We can become very behavioral and measure problems in terms of their frequency (how often does this occur?), intensity (how painful is it?) and duration (how long does it last?), and then set goals that indicate that any of these measures will decrease by a certain date. On the other hand we don't always have to be quite so specific. Some people just need to realize that they aren't going to live happily ever after.

Who Else Needs to Come Along on This Trip? The Inclusion of Interested Others.

Sometimes there are other people who can make a therapeutic journey easier. Not everyone has all the resources they need to get where they need to go and very few problems that people bring to us affect or involve them alone. Different schools of therapy have different "rules" about who should be included in the therapy sessions. Some family therapists insist on having all family members involved. Some individual therapists insist on seeing only the client. I suggest that we pay close attention to what our clients need instead of what the rules dictate. We can't assume that because we have included family members in a session that we are doing family therapy. Family therapy is a type of therapy practiced by those trained in family therapy and a process in which all of the family members are aware that they are involved in a therapeutic process.

When we pay close attention to our client's description of the problem we will soon figure out when and how others should be included. We can include anyone who might be helpful, remembering that each situation is unique and that no rule applies to all clients or to every situation. We do this by asking ourselves and our clients if there is anyone else who might be a part of the solution. Whenever we include others, however, we have to be very clear about why and how they are to be involved: the ground rules must be explicit. We can't invite someone in to help a spouse or a child and proceed to "do therapy" with that person. Further we also can't allow others to use the therapy session to tell tales about or to confront our clients.

I once had a family ask to come to therapy ostensibly to "help you learn more about our father." When I told them that I could not see them without my client's permission, they persuaded my client to invite them in for a session saying they wanted to do anything they could to help him. When they came, however, they used the session to criticize him and to try to persuade him to enter treatment for his chemical dependency. I was appalled by this and tried to mediate the situation and made it worse. My client felt deceived by his family and suspected that I knew their intentions. The family was incensed that I wouldn't join with them. The session was a disaster because neither the client nor I had any idea of what was about to happen. Everyone left the session feeling angry and dissatisfied. I was not in charge of the therapy session and therefore my client was not treated respectfully. I held myself responsible for that debacle and learned from that experience to set down the rules, make expectations clear and find out what "helpful" means before including others in the session.

As in most matters, common sense is better than theoretical dogma. Most parents who send their children to therapy should be actively involved in the therapy, but there are times when that involvement would be harmful to the child. Some children will speak freely when parents are around, and in other cases children need protection from abusing parents. In other cases the problem is so clearly a family problem that seeing the child on an individual basis will not be helpful unless it serves only to give the child a supportive oasis in a chaotic world. We can talk to parents about the difference between their *right* to know what their child is working on in therapy and their *need* to know all the details.

There may be other times we simply want a mate or a friend to come in for an informational or educational session or to normalize the process of therapy. One young adult client recently brought in her mother for a few minutes at the beginning of a session in order for her mother to meet me, see the office and feel more at ease about the whole process of therapy. Another client brings his grown sons to talk to me when they are in town so they can discuss their concerns about his ability to live independently.

Identifying Potential Roadblocks

Finally, before we start out on the road we can check for roadblocks. We ask the client, "What might keep you from reaching these goals?" And we ask, nicely, with genuine curiosity and without blame, how clients manage to stay stuck in the same place. If there are roadblocks, we can find out who can remove them and if there are people who are making it impossible for our clients to reach their objectives. Donald Meichenbaum has written extensively on patient compliance with medical advice. One of his questions to patients is, "What will prevent you from following the advice of the doctor?" Clients can't always answer these questions, but they are, if nothing else, a useful way to find out how our clients view their own situations.[7]

Mary
In Mary's case, at a crucial time in her therapy, her husband came to a session because he wanted information about what he could do when she became withdrawn and depressed. He had never known what to do when that happened and he had little knowledge of, in fact had always disapproved of, any sort of psychotherapy. Now, however, he was so dis-

> traught that he was willing to learn. Together, the three of us worked out a plan of action about what each of us would do when we became concerned about Mary and feared that she might try to kill herself. I believe that his willingness to come to a session was a visible sign of his caring that meant more to Mary than any words could have. If he had not been included he could have presented a substantial roadblock to her progress.

In summary, setting goals is a part of the assessment process and an integral element of psychotherapy. The goals should be achievable and whenever possible stated in behavioral terms so both therapist and client can know when they are reached. Goals can and do change during the course of therapy. Clients change direction. New goals are negotiated. However, we aren't being responsible to our clients or to ourselves when we drift along without objectives and goals. (Then, too, talking to clients about goals is especially helpful whenever you or the client feels stuck.)

Recommended Reading:

O'Hanlon's Field Guide, (O'Hanlon & Beadle, 1994) and Yvonne Dolan's *Resolving Sexual Abuse* (Dolan, 1991) contain examples of goal setting, specifying achievable goals, and quantifying vague goals, and suggesting possibilities. Dolan's book is especially helpful when working with victims of sexual abuse.

Meichenbaum, D.& Turk, D.C. (1987) *Facilitating Treatment Adherence: A Practitioner's Guidebook.* New York: Plenum Press presents practical methods of working with barriers and roadblocks.

Jongsma, A.E. & Turk, D.C. (1995) *The Complete Psychotherapy Treatment Planner.* New York: John Wiley and Sons is a useful book that describes problems, goals and objectives in behavioral terms. This book, and computerized treatment planners, save the therapist time when making maps that comply with standard diagnostic categories. I recommend it as a guidebook for making documented treatment plans to meet the demands of third party payers and to meet the required legal and ethical standard of various professional organizations on record keeping. Such treatment plans, however, do not begin to capture all the dimensions of good psychotherapy. We must not mistake the map for the territory.

Summary of Chapter Four

DECIDING ON A DESTINATION: SETTING GOALS IN THERAPY

PURPOSE OF GOALS IN THERAPY

- To resolve the complaint
- To recognize that enough progress has been made to stop therapy

ESSENTIALS OF ESTABLISHING GOALS

- Collaborate with the client
- Use magic wand and miracle questions to elicit clients's goals in video talk
- Identify Sub-goals (What is the first step or sign?)
- Negotiate solvable problems
- Identify others who can help
- Identify potential roadblocks

TECHNIQUES FOR MEASURING PROGRESS

- Self-scaling
- Quantifying time spent in having or not having the problem
- Identifying others who could measure progress

ASPECTS OF MEASURABLE GOALS IN THERAPY

- How often does the problem occur?
- When does the problem occur?
- How long does the problem last?

CHAPTER FIVE

Choosing the Proper Means of Transportation

In therapy there are no all-terrain vehicles

Many roads have the same destination.

An articulated, an all-worked-out psychology is better spoken of as a theology or a philosophy or a movement, and the activity performed in its name and called "therapy" (Freudian, Jungian, Rogerian, Reichean) is more truly indoctrination or conversion. It is more likely to be ideology than psychologizing. Perhaps there can be no discipline of therapeutic psychology, only an activity of psychotherapy.

James Hillman, *Revising Psychology*[1]

I never had a childhood. I had to take care of my younger brother and sister and never learned to play. I didn't even do the usual things kids do like learning how to swim.

Mary

How Are We Going to Get There? The Activities of Psychotherapy

Having found out where clients are and where they want to go, we begin to guide them toward their destinations. Devising therapeutic activities that are custom made for each client is the creative aspect of psychotherapy. Most activities we design will have been thought of before but they have not been applied by us in this specific situation. Each day is different, each client is different. Within the discipline of our profession there is ample room for creativity.[2]

If we aren't going to use the same methods for everyone, e.g., psychoanalysis, cognitive behavioral therapy, brief solution focused, or family therapy, how do we decide which activities to use? So far, I've suggested that we use different techniques to accomplish our own therapeutic tasks. Now we turn our attention to the client. What is going to be the best way to get this particular client where he or she wants to go? The way I propose in this book is that we identify a developmental task that this client has not yet accomplished, determine the inner resources (archetypes) that the client will need in order to accomplish that task, and then devise a therapeutic activity that will awaken those resources in that particular client.

The Process of Applied Archetypal Psychotherapy

Earlier I described the psychosocial stages devised by Erik Erikson as mileposts on the hero's journey. The completion of each of these stages involves two or more developmental tasks. The completion of these tasks is crucial to human psychosocial development. For example, the most troubled clients are ill-prepared for the journey and have not completed the developmental tasks of childhood. Their failure to do this shows itself in their inability to meet their own needs.

Therefore, people who were abused or abandoned before they could establish trust or autonomy frequently seek therapy because they are having difficulty sustaining significant relationships with others. Consequently, clients like Mary present with symptoms of dissociation, depression, and self injurious behaviors. These clients appear fearful, or angry and often describe episodes of dissociation. When clients like this learn to trust in their own ability to stand up for themselves (as Havens says, "Not to invade another or be invaded by another") and to care for and nurture themselves and not have to depend on others to do it for them, they are ready to take part in an adult relationship. If they do not accomplish these tasks, they will go through their lives engaging in a series of pseudo parent-child relationships. Relating to any form of authority is difficult when we haven't claimed authority over our own lives and are trapped in a state of dependency— a child-like state or one of continuous adolescent rebellion.

For that reason, when we determine that a client can neither nurture nor protect himself or herself we devise therapeutic activities designed to awaken the internal parents— the archetypes Pearson calls the Caregiver and the Warrior— who enable that client to develop the trust in self and the autonomy needed to move from a state of dependence to one of independence.

Consequently, to choose an appropriate therapeutic activity for a client we:
    1. Determine the stage of the journey on which a client's problem is found.
    2. Specify the developmental tasks related to that stage.

3. Identify the archetypal energies, or inner resources (and in some cases outer resources) that could enable the client to accomplish that task.
4. Choose a therapeutic activity to awaken that archetype in that particular client.

The charts in the chapter on Introduction to the Territory show the developmental tasks related to each stage of the journey and the archetypes that can be awakened to help accomplish these tasks. The following charts show how to determine the client's stage of the journey. We will use Mary's case as an example of this process.

Some Indications That the Client May Need to Develop Trust and Autonomy: Preparation for the Journey

The client is:
  Emotionally or physically dependent on others
  Describing herself as a victim.
  Distrustful and suspicious, or hyper-vigilant
  Angry, resentful and bitter: "Life is unfair and nothing good ever happens to me."
  Extremely concrete and literal; everything is seen in black or white
  Complaining of low self esteem.
  Or says, "I can't, I shouldn't, I'm afraid to be cause if I do he/she/they will."
  Or, is so suspicious or terrified that they say almost nothing and answer any question with, "I don't know."

> **Some Indications That the Client May Be Seeking Identity and Intimacy: The Journey**
>
> The client functions in the world and isn't being victimized or victimizing others but complains of:
> - Feeling alienated and lacking a sense of purpose or identity
> - An inability to commit to intimate relationships
> - Or, says, "I don't know what I want," or "I don't know what I want to do when I grow up!"
> - Or, says "I want," "I wish," "I always wanted to..."

> **Some Indications That the Problem May Concern the Return; the Development of Generativity and Integrity: The Return from the Journey**
>
> Although few clients come to us with problems in the return, those who do may complain of:
> - Problems integrating self into community (especially the work place)
> - Moral and ethical dilemmas
> - Workaholism
> - Inability to adapt to retirement
> - Lack of balance in their lives

Problems of the Journey and Return stages can appear at any time but *if autonomy and trust have not been developed, therapy will have to start there.* You can't take a journey until you have learned to cross the street by yourself and many psychotherapy clients are unprepared for the journey to individuation and beyond.

Working With Mary

The Caregiver and the Warrior are the archetypes necessary to prepare the Innocent and the Orphan to begin the journey. These were the inner resources that Mary needed to activate. Like many others, Mary was proficient in caring for others and also in fighting for the rights of others, but she was inexperienced in doing these things for herself. Thus, the focus of her therapy centered on the activities she needed to participate in to activate these archetypes.

Mary had to accomplish the developmental tasks of developing trust (in me, and ultimately in herself) and autonomy (the ability to take care of herself, emotionally and physically, and not depend on others to meet her emotional needs). As her therapist, my goal was to develop her capacity to care for herself, soothe herself, and stand up for herself. Mary was fond of the "inner child" metaphor so I began to look at these abilities or archetypes (Warrior and Caregiver) as her "inner parents."

Mary had many dragons. She held tightly to the belief that she must continue to "honor" her parents, which to her meant allowing her mother to lecture and criticize her for hours on the telephone and to acquiesce to her parents' demands for money to support her irresponsible siblings. At the same time, Mary had internalized the voice of her shadow Orphan that said that she was worthless, but she resented others for not understanding and loving her. In essence she was saying, "I want to be understood and loved by you but I despise myself, so don't ask me to love myself. I want you to love someone I consider worthless."

The therapeutic activities I chose were: being trustworthy and consistent, modeling limit setting, breaking the "bad trance"[3] that kept her frozen in time, teaching cognitive therapy techniques to handle intrusive thoughts, and devising assignments that changed her experience of herself in the present day world, such as asking her to join a therapy group and to learn to swim. In this chapter I'll describe two of these in detail: establishing trust by the therapist being trustworthy, and an assignment in the real world to awaken her Warrior and change her experience of herself.

Dragons have to be fought on the inside and the outside. Once clients begin to develop trust in themselves they can claim their personal authority by actually taking an action— doing something different— and thereby changing their own inner experience of themselves. There is a reciprocal relationship between trust in self and autonomy. Once we begin to assert ourselves we gain more and more trust in our own ability to take care of ourselves. Mary first had to develop enough trust in me that she would know that I wouldn't ask her to do something that would hurt her. For a long time she was suspicious of me, and of most other people, for life had taught Mary never to trust anyone.

Establishing Trust: Awakening the Caregiver
The most difficult therapeutic task I've encountered is the establishment of trust. It is, of course, possible in most cases to establish a trusting therapist/client relationship, but when a client has not yet learned to trust any caregiver it may take a long time to awaken the Innocent archetype. (Sadly, there are some whose early abuse or trauma was so extreme that they are not available for any kind of trusting relationship.)

Years ago when I worked as a therapist in a program for families in which there had been sexual abuse, I was assigned to facilitate a group of young victims and their siblings, ages six to twelve. These children were either wary, suspicious, and fearful, or surly and rebellious. I was to be their group therapist and meet with them for two hours each week while their parents were also in therapy. The children either feared authority or openly challenged it: either they sat quietly and did whatever they were told, or they ran all over the building. After several frustrating sessions I went to my supervisor in dismay and said, "How can I teach them to trust me?"

She smiled sadly, shook her head, and answered, "By being trustworthy."

These were wise words that took time and patience to put into practice. I had to respect the children and show them that I meant what I said. I couldn't worry about their liking me; I had to find things to like about each of them. I had to treat them like the children they were and find out about what they were interested in, teach them to play games and read them stories. These children taught me a great deal. I recognized that in two hours each week it was neither possible nor responsible for me to teach them to trust the adults in their world. Some of the most significant adults in their lives had betrayed them. They had been forced to grow up faster than other children, and they had to learn whom they could trust and whom they couldn't. Ultimately, of course, they would have to learn to trust themselves, but right now they were not able to take care of themselves. I forgot about what I was supposed to do and began to focus on what they needed— security, consistency and attention. I could give them this.

After that, for two hours each week they could trust me to take care of them, to protect them from harm, to show an interest in them, to listen to them, to provide some meaningful activity for them, set reasonable limits for them, and to be honest with them always. Again, I didn't need to "therapize" or "diagnose." I needed to find the children and be trustworthy in my dealings with them. I had to remember that there wasn't anything wrong with them, nor had they done anything wrong. There was something wrong with the parents who had abused their trust.

In the same way, that I had learned to work with these children I now needed to work to be a trustworthy therapist for Mary. There wasn't anything wrong with

Mary. I had to be firm and consistent and establish the parameters of the relationship (activate my own Warrior), and listen to her, and *experience the world through her eyes*. This took time. There was no reason why she should trust me, I had to earn her trust. I had to awaken Mary's Caregiver to teach her to take care of herself. Mary needed to trust me in the same way that the children had; to trust me to care for her during the hour she was with me; to be interested in her; to listen to her; and to teach her to take care of herself so that eventually she would not need me, or others, to take care of her in the future. Sharing my notes with Mary, as explained in a previous section, was one way I began to establish trust. This process took time because I often tried to go too fast and Mary would stop and I would have to go back and retrace my steps to find her again.

In addition to sharing my notes I had to learn to be truly genuine in the relationship. Mary was especially upset when I would go away on a trip. At first I tried to avoid or ignore her anger, but gradually, as she realized that I always returned when I said I would, she began to express her anger and irritation to me in words instead of actions or hostile stares, and we began to talk about this in our therapy sessions.

At first, she was only able to do this in a sarcastic way by saying something like, "I guess you're going away again on another trip and deserting your clients." However, when I could join her instead of defending myself, when I could hear and face her anger, and listen to her fears and complaints (and did not change my behavior as a result of them) we began to make progress. Mary became better able to state what she liked and didn't like— to assert herself— and I became better able to hear her. I began to awaken my Caregiver to take care of her instead of my Warrior to defend myself against her.

An important part of being trustworthy is being honest about one's own emotions and willing to deal with anger and fear in the therapy session. When I first began to work with Mary I was highly influenced by the prevailing notions of how to treat Borderline Personality Disorders and later the "party line" about how to treat victims of sexual abuse. I was often guarded in my responses to Mary and uneasy about setting limits (on what I regarded as her intrusiveness) because she was a victim.

At length I learned that we keep clients in a victim mode when we continue to do things for them that they are capable of doing themselves. I saw that I wasn't helping Mary by tolerating intrusive behavior or treating her like a child who had to be excused for acting badly. No one can ever make up to another for the childhood she didn't have, but not even a terrible childhood is an excuse for bad behavior. Mary's poor childhood was the reason that she hadn't learned what she should have learned,[4] and now she had an opportunity to learn these things in a safe environment. What I did need to do was to respect her and treat her well and expect her to act like the adult she was. Adults don't need parents, but therapists have to break this news very gently to some clients and respect the fact that many adults keep trying to get their parents (or their therapists) to love them as they wished they had been loved as a child.

Mary's childhood had indeed been brutal, and for a while I had felt myself trying to be the good mother that she never had. Ultimately I became aware that fulfilling Mary's expectations and doing good therapy were not the same thing. Mary didn't need a mother, she needed to learn to mother (and father) herself.

Encouraging Autonomy: Awakening the Warrior

Therefore, I began to plan the process of "teaching the birds to fly." If the nest were too comfortable, Mary might never want to leave. I initiated a series of what I call assignments in the real world. That is, therapy assignments that have a function in the therapy, that keep the client engaged in psychological work between sessions, and that also have a meaningful function in clients' daily lives. The purpose of these assignments is to change clients' inner experience of themselves and, in O'Hanlon's words, change the "doing" of the problem and of their lives. Such assignments also serve the function of making the client realize what she is capable of in the world she exists in today, as opposed to the restricted world of her childhood. Also, this is another way of breaking the trance of the Orphan and opening up access to resources and possibilities. This is another way to increase the usefulness of therapy when sessions are limited.

- **Awakening Mary's Warrior**

  Mary's next door neighbor, Olivia, had been a good friend for several years. Recently, however, when Olivia was offered a full- time job, she asked Mary to watch her two children for a few days until she could hire a permanent baby-sitter. The days dragged and became weeks, and now months. Mary was upset and felt used. She said nothing to her neighbor but talked in therapy about how upset she was.

  In the therapy session we began to develop Mary's Warrior by asking her to say the word "no" out loud and allowing herself to feel the physical change that took place in her body when she stood up straight and declared herself. Each time she did this she reported that she felt strong for a few minutes but quickly realized that she wasn't yet ready to stand up to Olivia, for soon after each practice she again felt deflated and powerless. This probably happened because Mary orphaned herself (turned her attention away from herself and toward her neighbor) and began to imagine how disappointed Olivia would be, or how angry she might be, and then to speculate about how Olivia might retaliate by telling others that Mary had let her down.[5]

Like most of us, Mary lost herself when she concentrated on the other person. It feels good to say "no" in a therapy session, but when faced with a spouse, or a parent, or even a good friend, it is not so easy for anyone to stand up for herself, let alone someone who has not yet achieved autonomy. Therefore, we devised a plan that helped her through this situation and started her on her way to claiming herself without totally alienating her neighbor. I asked Mary what she *would* be willing to do for Olivia. Mary thought for a while and said, "I will watch her children for one more week. After that I will also fill-in when emergencies come up. Other than that, I will not be available."

Mary rehearsed her lines then spoke to Olivia. She didn't back down when Olivia became angry and expressed her disappointment. By carrying out this assignment in the real world with an actual situation (in addition to a role play or imagery) Mary had a chance to experience herself differently. After years of determining her actions based on how others would react to her— reacting— Mary began to act. Instead of complaining to me (and others) about her inconsiderate neighbor, she had asserted herself. This small act of heroism, of saying yes to the self, started her on her way. Instead of saying "I can't do that because she will get angry," she was saying, "I can do this," and, "I will" and, "I won't."

Reluctantly Mary joined a therapy group that at first offered only support. She, too, at first was willing only to give and not take support from others. (For many who haven't awakened their internal Caregiver, it is much easier to give than to receive.) Initially, Mary interpreted any feedback as criticism. Gradually, however, the acceptance— the acknowledgment— of the group gave Mary the courage to begin to

> express herself and to allow other people to know her and to see and to tolerate her anger. After several painful encounters she learned to give and receive both feedback and support.
>
> Finally, Mary found a job. In her workplace she worked with a supervisor who placed unreasonable demands on her and faced many situations that in the past would have precipitated violent behavior, or deep depression, or self mutilation. Previously, a situation with an unreasonable authority figure would have recapitulated her relationship with her mother and sent her into a tailspin. Now, however, she stands up for herself and politely and firmly sets her own limits and takes responsibility for her actions. Today Mary is neither all right nor all wrong. She's a fallible human being who is becoming whole. She is no longer depressed. Now she fits neither the Borderline nor the PTSD diagnosis. She has survived and prevailed; and she has grown up. Mary's journey will continue every day of her life. She recognizes this as she continues to define herself and to stand up for her principles in her family and her community. Mary's journey continues but her therapy has ended.

Matching Intervention to Client and Situation: Three Depressed Clients

In Mary's case we saw a client unprepared for the journey. There isn't time or space to give extensive examples of the other stages of the journey, but the following brief vignettes show how similar problems manifest themselves in different stages of the journey.

People who are depressed and have never (or not yet) had the opportunity to see themselves as autonomous or independent beings, those whose depressed affect, and whose threats of suicide, have been their only way to get the attention they need, require first aid from the therapist in the form of directives and assignments. Sometimes they need medication and hospitalization.

Like parents, we must first safeguard our client (and others) before we can go on. When we have to intervene we are, in fact, acting in loco parentis— in place of parents— something we sometimes have to do to help a client prepare for the journey. Some clients first need to learn how to survive in the world.

On the other hand, a person whose depression is a call to find meaning and purpose in life will find behavioral, family therapy (or even medication) inadequate or intrusive. Although these clients may feel slightly better for a while, they will need more intensive inner work, using techniques like active imagination, flow writing, existential therapeutic conversations, clinical hypnosis, and dream work to delve into the depths of the imagination and explore yearnings, desires, and dreams. The answers these clients seek reside inside themselves and can be handled best by going inward.[6]

Examples: Three Depressed Clients
Susan is helpless (Stage 1)

Susan, a client with all of the symptoms of a major depression, is not yet prepared for the journey. She has a long history of depression. In fact, she can't remember when she wasn't depressed. Although she is an adult, she is dependent, financially and emotionally, on her parents. She is a college graduate but has no entry level job skills. She appears disorganized and acts helpless and reports that there are days when she does not get out of bed or brush her teeth or wash her face. Susan has many things to learn before she can begin her journey. Her depression might be characterized as a *"call for help."* She is not ready to begin the journey.

Susan has to learn to assert herself and to care for herself before her journey can begin. In her relationship with her therapist she will learn trust and ultimately develop the autonomy she needs to separate from her family and gain the psychological maturity to strike out on her own. The therapist's job is to find her and show her how to prepare for the journey. However, initially, the best vehicle for handling Susan's depression might be the emergency vehicle of medication. She may even need to be hospitalized before she can go on.

Jane has good ego strength but does not know what she wants out of life (Stage 2) Jane, who has the same symptoms, is far less dependent on others. Yet, she calls herself depressed, is sleepless, has lost her appetite, cannot concentrate on her work and feels alienated and rudderless in her life. However, her life is more in control than Susan's. Jane has a job, and maintains her own home. She has some ability to comfort herself and can remember that there have been times in her life when she wasn't depressed. Her depression might be better characterized as an existential crisis and explored as a *"call from the Gods."* A depressed client with good ego strength can delve more deeply into the feelings of depression in order to discover what is really important to her, find those parts of her life that have meaning, and let go of the parts that hinder her. The therapist will have to guide her inward to find what Keats called the "holiness of the heart's affections and the Truth of the Imagination."

Simon has good ego strength, knows what he wants, but is not getting it and is unhappy (Stage 3) Simon's depression, on the other hand, appears to be a reflection of the state of the world around him. The medical profession he once loved is now so regulated by others that he can no longer continue in his present job and provide ethical care to his patients. Simon must find ways to engage the world, take difficult steps, fight the system, and/or make major changes in his daily work and his life. Simon must claim the territory that is his, change what needs to be changed and enjoy what is his to enjoy. The therapist can guide him outward and support him in challenging the "world's fierce need to change him." His depression could be called a *"call to arms,"* and it would be a pity to give him a pill to get rid of it. A depressed person in the return phase of the journey may need, not so much to go inward as to go outward. The depression may be the call of the state of the world around him. He may have to change his relationship to the world— to apply his gifts to make changes in the world for the betterment of the community or the world or the ecology. The therapist's job is to affirm, encourage and guide him outward.

The therapist who is sensitive to the stage of the journey on which the client encounters depression will be better able to guide each client. Although we have to know about the various "treatments" of depression, we also have to determine the best treatment for each client in the context of that client's life. Anti-depressants may be necessary for Susan until she learns how to take care of herself (and maybe even after that) but anti-depressants could postpone the journey for Jane and for Simon. The therapist/guide must know when to relieve the pain and when to follow the intensity of the pain down the rabbit hole into and out of the wonderland.

Remember, we don't need to be restricted to the theory of the etiology of the problem, condition, or concern to find the therapeutic task that will help your client to reach a goal. Even though I believe in Jung's theories of the collective unconscious as a reservoir of residual strengths, and believe in individuation as the destination of the hero's journey, and believe in psychological types as inherent differences in the ways that we perceive and interact with the world around us, I don't need to limit myself to the procedure of Jungian analysis (nor am I qualified to) in order to help my client find his or her path.

Techniques from different schools of therapy can be used as complements to each other. "Dragons," for instance, can be seen as musts or shoulds, introjects, or even a "bad trance." Dragons can be externalized by the narrative method,[7] attacked by Rational Emotive Therapy[8] or cognitive restructuring,[9] and eliminated (slain) by "de-hypnotizing."[10] Behavioral prescriptions can be used to awaken the Warrior and the Caregiver within. Age regression and age progression can help clients to heal wounds and find meaning in painful experiences. Family therapy and consultation in the workplace can enable the returning hero to share treasures with the kingdom. Metaphor, storytelling, and dream work and Jungian inner work create pathways for the soul journey. However, don't mistake this as a cookbook approach, e.g., psychodynamic approaches for ego problems, Jungian dream work for soul journeys. The course of the therapy depends on the demands of the individual path of each hero and the skill of the guide. Any activity can be used with any problem at any stage of the journey so long as we have *found the client,* we *keep the client's goals and best interests in mind,* and so long as *we know why we have chosen to use that technique.*

A good rule to remember is O'Hanlon's rule: "Go with what is compassionate and respectful, and what works. And remember, no matter how typical or stuck or hopeless a client may seem, *everybody is an exception!"*[11]

Recommended Reading:

For additional information on making a treatment plan see Jongsma, A.E. & Peterson, M.L.(1995) *The Complete Psychotherapy Treatment Planner.* New York: John Wiley and Sons, Inc.

For therapeutic activities see Robert Johnson's *Inner Work,* (Johnson, 1986) (San Francisco: Harper and Row) and Nicole Ricoís *Pain and Possibility: Writing Your Way Through Personal Crisis* (Rico, 1991) (Los Angeles: Jeremy Tarcher). Harriet Lerner's (1985) *The Dance of Anger*, New York: Harper and Row is a classic and one of the most helpful books a therapist can use to help clients understand the nature of anger and what they can do about it.

Summary of Chapter Five

THE 4-STEP PROCESS OF APPLIED ARCHETYPAL PSYCHOTHERAPY

1. DETERMINE THE STAGE OF THE JOURNEY
- The Stages of the Hero's Journey
- Stage One: Preparation for Separation— Dependence, Ego Building
- Elements:
  The Call, the Fall, Wounds, Facing the Dragons

- Stage Two: The Journey to Find the Individual— Independence, Soul Finding
- Elements:
  Fighting the Dragons and Finding the Treasure

- Stage Three: The Return to Community— Interdependence — Self Responsibility
- Elements: Sharing the Treasure with Others

2. IDENTIFY THE DEVELOPMENTAL TASK TO BE ACCOMPLISHED
Stages of the Journey and Erikson's Psychosocial Stages and Tasks
- Preparation — ego development— dependence
  - trust: task = developing trust in self and others
  - autonomy: task = developing the ability to stand up for, protect and defend the self
  - initiative: task = learning to take responsibility for self
  - industry: task = learning basic social skills and work habits

- Journey — soul — identity, independence
    - identity: task = finding what you love, creating, and letting go
    - intimacy: task = finding whom you love, willingness to commit and let go
- Return — self — wholeness, interdependence
    - generativity: task = actively sharing your gifts with others
    - integrity: task = being true to yourself and claiming your own wisdom

3. IDENTIFY THE ARCHETYPES TO AWAKEN

Stages of the Journey and Erikson's Psychosocial Stages/Tasks

- Preparation: ego development — dependence

Archetypes	Tasks
Innocent	trust
Orphan	autonomy
Caregiver	industry
Warrior	initiative

- Journey: soul — identity, independence

Archetypes	Tasks
Seeker	identity
Lover	intimacy
Creator	
Destroyer	

- Return: self — wholeness, interdependence

Archetypes	Tasks
Ruler	generativity
Sage	integrity
Magician	
Jester	

4. SELECT ACTIVITIES TO AWAKEN THOSE ARCHETYPES

These are merely suggestions— all therapies can work at any level
- Metaphor and story telling at all levels

To Awaken Ego Archetypes:
- Action and movement: role play, direct assignments, solution oriented and possibility therapy, family therapies
- Imagery: Competent self returning to trauma and caring for or protecting young and vulnerable self, clinical hypnosis and breaking trance and healing trance

- Interaction: therapist example and transference, narrative therapy

To Awaken Soul Archetypes:
- Imagery: Guided imagery, clinical hypnosis, journal and flow writing, dream analysis, Jungian analysis, metaphor, and story telling

- Action and movement: art therapy, journal and poetry writing, dance

- Interaction: Existential and humanistic therapies

- Transpersonal therapies: All

To Awaken the Archetypes of the Return
- Action and movement: Psychoeducational therapies. Reality therapy, treatment for sexual

disorders and chemical dependency, family and systems therapies

- Imagery: to enhance any other forms of therapy and envision better ways of interacting with the world

- Interaction: Group therapies, systems therapies, narrative therapy

- Transpersonal: Body/mind therapies, therapies to raise the consciousness of the world

CHAPTER SIX

Following the Rules of the Road

Keep all vehicles up to date, use properly licensed drivers, and obey the rules of the road.

The Professional Journey Guide

Most ethical concerns in psychotherapy concern the client-therapist relationship. Yet, as we know, different schools advise different ways to relate to the client. How do we reconcile different approaches to the therapist/client relationship? We begin with a discussion of the nature of the professional relationship itself.

The Nature of Professionalism: Therapy is not a Social Event

When I refer to psychotherapists as Journey Guides, and talk about archetypes, myths, heroes, dragons, the call, and the fall, I don't mean to suggest that we abandon our professionalism. I may depart from traditional title and language, but as a psychotherapist I have a profound professional obligation to my clients. Buckman explains the professional relationship as follows:

> ...the professional relationship contains an implicit contract between the healthcare professional and the patient that is absent in social interactions. The contract is based on

> the fact that the professional... has access to knowledge and expertise that puts him or her at an advantage over the patient. The codes of all medical professions are based on the understanding that the professional partner will not use that knowledge to the disadvantage of the patient or client. In other words, the potential vulnerability of the patient is protected by the code of professional behaviour incumbent on the professional person...the professional person is obliged to use his or her professional abilities for the benefit of the patient (the concept in medical ethics of "beneficence"). This obligation limits the number of options available to you...being professional means that we have to honor certain obligations to our patients.[1]

Although Buckman speaks to the medical professions his words pertain to psychotherapy as well. On the other hand, Hillman claims that the professional relationship itself hampers the effectiveness of psychotherapy:

> How can we take back therapy from the killing asymmetry of professionalism and the political abuses of wrong pathologizing, from a system which must find illness in order to promote health and which in order to increase the range of its helping, is obliged to extend the area of sickness. Ever deeper pockets of pathology to be analyzed, ever earlier traumata: the family, the office force, community mental health, analysis for everyone.[2]

I sympathize with Hillman. I, too, am upset by

"wrong pathologizing" and the medicalization of psychotherapy, but what if the difficulty is not in the way we expand the definition of pathology but in the way we define professionalism? To be a professional is, of necessity, to have an asymmetrical relationship with our clients. There is nothing intrinsically wrong with asymmetry so long as the professional recognizes an ongoing responsibility to adhere to the principle of beneficence— to think first of what is good for the client. The problem for psychotherapists may not lie in the asymmetrical relationship between therapist and client but, instead, in the application of one method— in the above case, analysis— to every client and every situation. I suggest that we adjust the professional relationship according to the task we are trying to accomplish and the stage of the journey on which the client is found, and use methods that best accomplish our goals.

- **Maintain a Flexible Therapist-Client Relationship**

Most of the change that takes place in psychotherapy occurs because of the relationship between therapist and client. Our credentials endow us with authority and with serious responsibility.[3] Clients acknowledge this authority, entrust us with their deepest secrets, and share with us their greatest fears. They listen to our every word and often take us very literally. (They sometimes hear things we never remember having said.) We have the potential to do great harm when we do not respect and uphold the professional relationship. At times this relationship feels like a warm personal friendship. Nonetheless, even though a client might mistake a therapeutic relationship for a friendship, we therapists can never make this error. The professional therapist takes responsibility for the well-being of clients and doesn't overstep the bounds of professional ethics, all of which are explicitly spelled out by the governing boards that license psychologists, psychiatrists, social workers, counselors, and pastoral counselors. These are the rules of the road.

Nonetheless, it is never possible to set forth a group of rules that tell us the best thing to do in every situation with every client. For example, because there are so many different schools of psychology, there is no general agreement about the exact nature of the therapeutic relationship. Therefore, although it is easy to know whether or not one should have a romantic or sexual relationship with a client, it is not so easy to say whether or not (or under what circumstances) a therapist should disclose personal information, state an opinion, give advice, or take a position on a question of morality. Unlike Colleen, who searched in vain to discover the rules for every situation, we have to rely on our own good judgment; and judgment calls are difficult to make.

Each school of psychotherapy views the relationship of client and therapist in a different light. The psychodynamic school prescribes a relationship of therapist to client as a transference relationship that provides a receptacle in which the unresolved issues of parent and child can be worked through. Psychoanalysts analyze and interpret a client's work but don't disclose personal information or give any directives to the client. The behaviorist schools, and many schools of family therapy and action oriented therapies, put the therapist in the role of a trainer or strategist in which the personal relationship of client to therapist is minimized and the notion of transference is not discussed. The existentialist-humanist schools, on the other hand, emphasize the relationship between therapist and client and advise the therapist to meet the client as a fellow human in a non-judgmental genuine encounter with "unconditional positive regard." Each role carries with it different responsibilities for the therapist.

Both Freud and Jung considered transference ("the process by which strong positive or negative feelings... are transferred from the person in the patient's life who occasioned them, to the psychoanalyst")[4] to be the most important factor in the therapy. But, those of us who don't see our function as analytical might be more comfortable with Yalom's notion of a "real" relationship between client and therapist. Yalom states,"There is enormous potential benefit in the patient's developing a real (as opposed to a transferential) relationship to the therapist. Rather than the relationship being an "as if" phenomenon — one that analyzed properly will facilitate other relationships — the therapist helps to heal by developing a genuine relationship with the patient."[5,6]

Each school has a valid point of view. For that reason, I propose that when we cast the client in the role of hero we ask the therapist to be capable of assuming each of these roles when they are called for. We can choose the proper relationship to the client on the basis of the specific needs of the client at that moment in time rather than adhere to an approach determined by a particular theoretical orientation. This requires flexibility and good judgment. We have to know when to be parental, when to "meet the other" in a genuine human encounter, when to analyze and interpret and when to be strategic, directive, active, goal oriented, and even when to take the responsibility to act as an agent of society.[7] The relationship between therapist and client can, and often does, change during the course of therapy with each individual.

- **Determine who the client is: Who *is* the client?**

Sometimes it is difficult to know exactly who the client is. When we agree to work with someone we have to be clear in our own minds about who that someone is. We also have to be sure that everyone has the same goals in mind. This can be particularly perplexing when we work with children or adolescents, clients ordered by the court to go to therapy, and managed care (which someone has suggested should be called managed costs). I don't have all the answers to this but I believe we have to keep asking, "Who is the client?"

Very often we are called in to satisfy *multiple customers with different agendas,* so we better make sure at the start who has hired us, who can fire us, and whether there are any ethical or legal considerations that may constrain us or affect the therapy. O'Hanlon asks, "Who is complaining?" "Who is alarmed about something?" "Who is paying?" "Who will be able to terminate therapy?" [8]

- **Therapy and society**

Another consideration is the difference between treatment and therapy. For example, I once worked as a group facilitator in a treatment program for convicted sex offenders. When I began this program I thought that the offenders were my clients but soon realized that these "clients" were neither determining the agenda of the group, nor setting the goals, nor were they paying me. I wasn't acting as a therapist, I was an agent of a treatment program. Therefore, in this case, the community corrections agency (society) was my client. I had a professional relationship and responsibility to the men in the group, but their needs did not come first; the needs of society came first.

I now make a distinction between treatment and psychotherapy. In psychotherapy, a client is the central focus of the therapist who is trying to help that client to find "True North" or help a family resolve a problem. The client or the family determines the agenda. In treatment, someone else sets the agenda and decides when a client has successfully completed a program. There is not a collaborative relationship between therapist and client, and the program is designed by someone other than the client. In the sex offender group I was responsible to community corrections; my co-facilitator and I set the agenda for the group, and we were paid by the county. As a psychotherapist in private practice, however, the women in my therapy group are my clients. They decide what to talk about in group, determine their own goals— and they pay the fee. (Although when their bills are paid by a third party I also have certain responsibilities to those payers and there are times when the best interests of the client and the requirements of the third party payers are in conflict. What is my responsibility, for example, when I have agreed to work with a client and believe that he or she needs more sessions and the insurance company denies my request for those sessions?)

There are other situations in which society as a whole can be considered as the client and the needs of the person we are working with take second place. Society is the client when we are bound by law to report suspicion of the abuse of children and vulnerable adults, or when we are obligated to disclose information to parents when working with their minor children, or required to disclose information that one of our clients plans to inflict bodily harm on another person. These situations are not always clear-cut and often require consultation with supervisors and boards of ethics in order to determine the proper course of action. Even then, we may sometimes ask ourselves if what we are doing is in the best interest of the client or whether we are doing something to prevent being sued.

Fortunately, most ethical dilemmas can be avoided when the therapist and the client clarify goals, obligations, and expectations at the very beginning of the their work together. This is what Dr. Lochland Farrow[9] refers to in the medical world as "preventive ethics." Farrow contends that ethical dilemmas are more easily avoided when we get to know our patients and clients well, when we have clearly described to them what we can and cannot do, and when we know what it is that they want and expect.

How to Keep Ourselves From Getting Lost

Therapy is a journey taken by therapist and client, a journey that delves deeply into the world as perceived and experienced by the client. But this type of quest demands that therapists also be in contact with their own phenomenological world.

Gerald Corey

It's easy to get lost and find ourselves doing our own therapy instead of concentrating on our client's needs. Consequently we need to expand our methods of keeping ourselves on track and staying in touch with our own phenomenological world. Proper therapy supervision, in addition to case consultation, is a good way to stay on track.

Supervision

A mark of a professional is that he or she continues to learn from personal experience. In our field we have ample opportunity to do so when we avail ourselves of therapy supervision. In supervision we can see ourselves as others see us. We can get an objective view of our relationship to our clients. I know of no other field with this particular advantage. Although most agencies and institutions provide therapy supervision for their employees, therapists in private practice have the responsibility to seek out and pay for their own. No matter how skilled or experienced we become, we have to find, or create peer supervision groups when no one provides them for us.

- **Self supervision**

In addition to supervision, I use a process of self supervision that was an outgrowth of my work with Mary. When I wrote my notes for Mary I recapitulated everything I remembered about the session. Then I analyzed the session as if I were supervising someone else. I wrote comments to myself and made suggestions about things I might have overlooked and questions I wanted to ask in the next session. Although I wrote these notes to Mary, they proved so useful to me that I have continued to write similar notes about my work with other clients. I don't always share these notes with my clients, but I make them available for clients who want them. The greatest value of these notes is that they help me keep myself on track. Very often in the course of writing I become aware of something I didn't notice in the session.

> Here is an example of a self supervising note:
> One other thing she said needs to be explored, "I was glad when my husband went back on the road because I didn't have to pretend any more that everything is all right. He gets so upset when I am anxious that I have to pretend around him. I can't let him know that I'm anxious." (My comment: Each day she lives out the childhood experience of covering up her own feelings and not upsetting others. I missed the significance of this when she said it so casually at the end of the session. I have to come back to this and explore what it is like for her to have to continue to pretend. I have to find out what she wants to do about this and design activities to help her. Not pretending— being herself with him— may be the very activity she needs to bring her into the present time instead of continuing to re-live her life the way she did as a child. What is she pretending with me?)

- **Client supervision**

Anthony Stevens, an eminent writer and Jungian analyst, in addition to requiring his clients to keep a detailed dream notebook, also asks his clients to take notes during and sometimes after each session to provide an ongoing record of their therapy.[10] In the course of my own psychotherapy I summarized each session when I returned home and paid close attention to the things that I had carefully avoided mentioning. I talked about these matters at the next session. In my practice I have also used session evaluation forms for group therapy that ask clients what they avoided talking about and what they found most helpful in that session.

Continuing education

An additional mark of professionals in any field is that they never stop learning. When our learning ceases, or our minds close, we are no longer eligible to be called professionals. Fortunately, there are many opportunities for us to continue learning. There are exceptional theorists and accomplished therapists alive today who write good books, produce educational videotapes, and present workshops all over the country. We can go to workshops and classes, read the books, and watch the videos. Workshops, often lively and fun, are sometimes held in attractive places where we can combine business with pleasure. There is no rule that says we have to suffer when we are learning.

Recommended Reading:

There are dozens of good journals and hundreds of excellent books about psychotherapy published each year, but it is difficult to keep up with all of them. It is a good idea to join professional organizations and read their journals [psychologists can read the APA (American Psychological Association) Monitor and the state Psychological Association magazines]. I have found The Family Therapy Networker magazine readily available and highly readable. It provides well written articles and commentary on current concerns and controversies in the field, and timely information about training and workshop opportunities all over the country.

A useful resource for the clinician is *Innovations in Clinical Practice*, a multi-volume collection of practical articles, published yearly by the Professional Resource Press, PO Box 15560, Sarasota, FL 34277-1560. The authors give permission to copy and share their forms with friends or to use them for educational purposes.

I recommend five books for guidance on the therapist/ client relationship:

Sheldon Kopp (1977) *Back to One: A Practical Guide for Psychotherapists*. Palo Alto, CA: Science and Behavior Books.

James Bugental (1987) *The Art of the Pychotherapist*. New York: W.W. Norton and Company.

Leston Havens (1986) *Making Contact: Uses of Language in Psychotherapy*. Cambridge, MA: Harvard University Press.

Anthony Storr (1990) *The Art of Psychotherapy*. New York: Routledge.

William O'Hanlon (1996) *The Handout Book*. Omaha, NE: Possibility Press, contains handouts that can be used in the daily practice of psychotherapy including office forms and information on how to determine who the client is.

Summary Chart of Chapter Six

THE RULES OF THE ROAD

- Professionalism: Therapy is not a social event
- Maintain a flexible professional relationship
- Know the needs of your client
- How to keep yourself from getting lost
  - Never stop learning
  - Supervision
  - Client supervision
  - Continuing education
  - Ask yourself questions

SIX FINAL REMINDERS FOR THE GUIDE

1. Don't let your clients out of your sight

2. If you get lost, ask for directions

3. Don't lead a client into territory when you don't know the way out

4. You are in charge of the expedition but not in charge of your clients's lives

5. Do the best you can with what you have; resources aren't infinite

6. Know when your part of the journey is over and it's time for a client to continue on alone.

CHAPTER SEVEN

Applying the Archetypal Model

Practical examples of what it's like to work with Innocents and Orphans

---

　　Eugenia, a handsome statuesque woman, well groomed and elegantly dressed, leans forward in her chair; her tears carry rivers of black mascara down her cheeks. She pauses to blot carefully with a tissue, then turns to me and asks, "Why is this happening to me?" After twenty years of what I thought was a happy marriage, Allen has left. I followed all the rules. I did everything right. I was good and I failed. No wonder he left me, look at how I look. I have no will power and can't lose weight. I haven't even been able to work at my art since he left. Why did he leave? How could I have failed so miserably when I thought I was being so good?

● ● ● ● ● ● ● ● ● ● ● ● ● ●

　　Maria sits on the edge of her chair breathing shallowly and rapidly. Large red blotches appear on her face and neck and tears well in her eyes. She sobs, "This isn't the way I expected my life to be! This isn't what I want. I want to be happy and have friends who support me and encourage me. I went home from work and cried myself to sleep because no one is doing anything to support me or to change my unethical work environment."

● ● ● ● ● ● ● ● ● ● ● ● ● ●

Clarence is a successful lawyer but in my office he looks like a confused little boy as he talks about his difficulties raising his two adolescent sons. He says, "Tell me the rules. Why doesn't someone write the regulations about this. If someone will just tell me what to do I can do it, but I don't know the rules about relating to my kids and they aren't turning out the way I expected them to."

● ● ● ● ● ● ● ● ● ● ● ● ● ●

Peggy complains to all of her friends (and her therapist) about Ben's insensitivity to her needs. However, she is hesitant to tell him. She complains, "I can't tell him how I feel or what I want from him because if I do, he will get angry and when he gets angry he may leave"

What's going on here? Again and again competent, successful, well-educated people ask therapists to tell them the rules; to tell them what to do so that they will be cared for, supported, or that things will turn out the way they expected. The questions seem to be, "How can I get someone else to meet my expectations?" "What are the rules? I thought I knew the rules but others aren't playing by them."

Why is this? How does it happen that people who can function well in every other area of their lives have difficulty maintaining their most significant interpersonal relationships? Therapists label these clients Dependent Personality Disorders, Borderline Personality Disorders, Histrionic or Narcissistic Personality Disorders but I have learned to think of these clients as lost and to realize that I can find them, help them decide where they want to go and figure out the best way to get them there. We begin with the Innocent.

> # Working with Innocents: The Story of Ruth
>
> Example: Ruth
> Assessment: low level Innocent, orphaned from her own feelings
> Developmental tasks: Learning to survive and relate to the outside world, developing autonomy, and accepting "the fall"
> Therapeutic tasks: Awaken Caregiver and Warrior
> Therapeutic activities: Breaking the bad trance
> Therapist's lesson: Breaking the therapist's trance
> (countertransference)

Return to the Innocent

As a beginning therapist I was surprised at how many women (and some men) in therapy bemoaned the fact that the world wasn't the way they were told that it would be and that life was so unfair. They expected to live happily ever after because they had done all the right things. They were deeply concerned with the unfairness of life and acted as if there were a judge somewhere (the therapist perhaps) who would make the right pronouncements. At first I thought I could use cognitive behavioral therapy with these clients and help them see their erroneous beliefs and cognitive distortions. Sometimes this worked, and I still think it a good place to start, but it doesn't work when the client is one who must learn from experience rather than from changing cognitions. Some have to change the "doing" before they can change the "viewing."[1]

Over the years, I've learned from my students, my clients, and my own children that not all people learn things in the same way. Some people are able to learn things intellectually, internalize information, and learn from others' mistakes. Others have to learn from their own experience. A purely cognitive approach doesn't allow the Innocent to experience the "fall." God didn't explain to Adam and Eve that it would be necessary for them to leave the garden of Eden. He kicked them out! They felt it. Today, I consider clients like these as Innocents and help them accept the fall and feel the inevitable grief and despair that comes with disillusion and deception. Through the process of accepting and surviving the fall, Innocents discover their own strengths and learn that they can survive without protectors.

Lost and found: the client isn't the only one who can get lost.

I saw Ruth for a long time before I realized that I was contributing to her problem rather than helping her. Ruth, a childless, married woman in her early forties, came to therapy several years ago complaining of depression, and a lack of a sense of purpose. She found her job boring and wanted to find the career that she was "meant for." She said she worked hard to help her friends and exhausted herself in the process. Ruth considered sacrifice to be her most positive attribute. She described herself as a "people person, a true care-taker, who cares more about others than I do about myself."

However, Ruth's primary complaint was depression. Whenever she had a serious argument with her husband and feared that he might leave she would cry for days and beg her husband to stay home with her because she was afraid of what she might do if she were left alone. Her goals— or rather hopes— for therapy were to have the depression lift, improve her relationship, find her ideal career. Because this was a tall order and her husband wasn't there, we began with the depression.

When I first met Ruth I was an advocate of Cognitive therapy and designed my treatment plan accordingly. The cognitive intellectual approach to therapy made both of us comfortable and our discussions were interesting and informative. (I should have realized that we were too comfortable.) Nonetheless, Ruth's depression lessened and after a while she stopped therapy. A few years later she returned because of recurrent episodes of depression. When, after several months of therapy, her mood didn't change and her problems weren't resolved, she consulted a psychiatrist who prescribed Prozac.® Ruth felt better almost immediately. She proclaimed Prozac® to be magic and again she terminated therapy.

Losing the client

During the time that Prozac® seemed to be the solution and things were going well, Ruth's husband, Sam, who was also contemplating a career change, took an apartment of his own. He claimed he wanted his own "space" and felt that each of them might better work out their destinies if they weren't together day and night. I was surprised at Ruth's acceptance of this. However, she agreed that she, too, needed time alone, saying "I need time to work on myself. I can't have my whole life revolve around him." I was relieved, this was what I wanted to hear. Ruth seemed better and for about a year I seldom saw her. Occasionally, she would come in for an appointment and complain about Sam and his life style and his new friends whom she criticized and resented, saying, "He has time for them but not for me." I wasn't able to get her to talk about herself or to identify what she needed. It seemed that she was living Sam's life instead of her own. She explored other job opportunities at this time but always with an eye on what would fit with Sam's plans. I worried, but couldn't seem to reach her. Then came the crisis.

One day Sam called to ask her to return the keys to his apartment. He had asked another woman to move in with him and wanted his privacy. Ruth, shocked and horrified, came back to therapy complaining, "All of my life I have done the right thing and other people have let me down time after time. I have been the good girl and I get punished for it while others get away with outrageous behavior. I want to make him see that I have been wronged. I shouldn't have to be suffering like this. This is too hard. I want to kill myself. Life isn't worth living if it is like this. First my parents let me down and now this. Why does this happen to me? I am not a bad person. Why am I being punished?"

Although Ruth never mentioned it to me, throughout their separation she had continued to clean, cook, and shop for Sam hoping that he would see how much he depended on her and come back to her. She remained at his beck and call and whenever he needed help or when he was lonely, he called her. The time she claimed she had taken to "work on herself" (whatever that means) she had spent becoming an expert on his needs and his insufficiencies. Ruth was furious at the other woman but not with Sam. "I can't get angry at him," she said, "because when he sees that he's done the wrong thing, and when he sees how shallow and manipulative that woman is, and when he realizes how much I have done for him, then he'll come back to me."

At first, overtaken by my own Caregiver archetype and surprised at her reaction (after all, he'd been gone for two years), I responded with kindness and concern. I continued to see her and respond to her frequent phone calls asking me to explain what had happened and to reassure her that she would be all right. However, when I insisted that she talk about herself and not Sam she became annoyed and reminded me that there was no one else she could talk to about this. She accused me of abandoning her and not being supportive. I wanted to be thought of as the kindly therapist and I was also frightened by her statements that she didn't want to go on living so I continued to respond to her. Even though Sam had left and was now living with someone else, she continued to talk to me about him and what he was doing wrong. She held to the belief that if she could convince him of the error of his ways he would see that she was right, and that she was indispensable! She maintained, quite rightly, that no one would ever be able to do as much for him as she had done.

One day, however, she called me at home at a most inconvenient time, interrupting an important transaction. That week in supervision, when asked about my reaction to her call, I realized that even though I had been annoyed at the interruption, I had paid no attention to my own feelings and merely tried to reassure my client and be a good mother to her. I then expressed my anger to my supervisor instead of changing what I was doing with my client. I talked about my client instead of talking to her which was exactly what she was doing in therapy— talking to me about Sam instead of dealing with Sam himself.

I was recapitulating in therapy the exact relationship Ruth had with her husband. I was being "good" and doing all the "right things" according to my own rules about being "nice" and supportive and was thereby keeping Ruth in a dependent relationship with me (something I deplored in other therapists, which should have alerted me that it might be my own problem). Fearing that she then would feel abandoned by me, as well as all the others in her life, I led her on by not risking a fight or a confrontation. I was thinking about what she would think of me instead of joining her and staying with her through her pain. I had lost her and needed to find her again.

Looking at theories instead of facing facts

I lost her when I looked away from her and to my theories and didn't see that she, too, was looking at her theories instead of facing facts. I looked at where I wanted her to be instead of where she was. It is a major mistake in tennis to look where you want the ball to go instead of where it is, for to do this, you have to take your eye off the ball. In the same way that I lost at tennis, I had lost my client.

Re-finding the therapist's self

Before I could find Ruth, I had to find myself. I needed to re-visit my ideas about therapy and theory and clarify what I was trying to do and trying to help others to do. All of us— both clients and therapists— are bombarded daily by conflicting theories and explanations of human behavior. Like my clients, I was trying to do the right thing and it wasn't working. I needed to stop and face the facts; to stand still.

When I found the hero's journey model I returned to Ruth as a guide, seeing Ruth and my relationship to Ruth, in a different light. Ruth was an Innocent, unprepared for the journey, unable to claim her own life. My task as her guide was to find her, help her decide on her destination, and find the proper vehicle to get her there. I didn't need to be her parent; I had to teach her to be her own parent.

Returning to Ruth: The Innocent

The magnificent gift of the Innocent archetype is the ability to trust, hope and have faith. But the Innocent who comes into therapy is frozen in a state of innocence and, therefore, has too much trust, hope and faith. Although shadow Innocents may be exceptionally competent in most areas of their lives, in significant interpersonal relationships they function as dependent children who need to enlist other people to take care of them and tell them the right thing to do. (They personify the dreadful term co-dependency.) The Innocent has not faced the "fall."

From the viewpoint of the hero's journey, Ruth was unprepared. She lived in a state of Innocence believing that if only she tried hard enough people would do the right thing, and that if they didn't, it was because she hasn't been good enough. Ruth's behaviors, both with me and in her relationship with Sam, were directed at persuading us to take care of her. To do this she used the same methods she employed as a child: she whined, she cajoled, she argued, she questioned, and intellectualized, believing that she could make things turn out if only she tried hard enough. Ruth used the same techniques to get me to take care of her to as she had to persuade Sam to take care of her, and up to now, I had obliged.

Now I could see that Ruth was terrified of being abandoned— the most traumatic of all childhood fears: the first and most intense pain a child suffers. To an infant or young child abandonment means death. Children instinctively know they will die if their parents leave them. In insecure children the emotional state activated by separation anxiety creates patterns that become the "prototypes for later interactions involving attachment and loss." [2] From then on, those who have not learned to care for themselves may experience all later leavings as abandonment— an experience as intense as any life threatening situation. Those who are abandoned later in life realize that they can survive suffering, but those who haven't yet faced the fall are unaware that they can survive loss and pain. Children can't take on their own suffering and pain and face the reality of the fall because they literally cannot survive without parents. Ruth was no longer a young child, but she was feeling this pain as intensely as a child, and I was treating her as a child.

All along I thought I could spare her suffering, but now I wondered if I had done this for her sake or mine. Thinking that we were not working on transference, I'd forgotten about countertransference! Now, I needed to find her. I didn't need to learn more about how to treat depression, or personality disorders, or how to do marriage counseling, I needed to figure out what Ruth had to learn or to do, in order to start living her own life and making her own choices. Then I had to create a therapeutic activity or intervention in which she would have the opportunity to do what she needed to do.

> The developmental task: Learn to survive and relate to the outside world by developing the autonomy to accept "the fall"
> The therapeutic task: awaken Caregiver and Warrior within the client
> The therapeutic activity: Breaking the bad trance.

The Trance of the Innocent

Ruth had fallen into the trance of the Innocent. In a trance state, "consciousness, like a shaft of light in a dark room, becomes acutely aware of some things while blind to others."[3] While our attention is focused in one direction other assets or archetypes are unavailable to us. When Ruth focused on the belief that if she worked hard enough she could get what she wanted, she was literally out of touch with her other inner resources and with the reality of the situation. She stated repeatedly that she couldn't believe what was happening. And each time she said this she seemed to regress in age to a time when she literally could not take care of herself.

- **Casting the spell**

There are many ways to look at the symptoms that bring people into therapy. Psychiatrists view them as pathology to be eliminated, medicated or cured. The archetypal psychologist, James Hillman, considers symptoms and pathologies as "calls from the Gods" to be attended to but not medicalized. Cognitive therapists call them erroneous beliefs or cognitive distortions. Stephen Wolinsky, on the other hand, conceptualizes symptoms as "clusters of trance phenomena" and he uses therapy to break the bad trance.[4]

Wolinsky claims that trances are created in childhood in response to threat and *"become sources of pathology* as they are integrated into the child's habitual mode of response." By the time adulthood is reached these responses have become "intricate patterns of defense woven out of clusters of Deep Trance phenomena that appear to function autonomously within us."[5]

Children are good hypnotic subjects and use self induced trances to cope with experiences they can't integrate or tolerate. They will, for example, dissociate from sexual abuse or develop amnesia for many types of trauma. These are natural coping mechanisms that serve to protect a child, but become symptoms in adulthood when they are the only way that person can cope or respond to stress. Once the trance is broken a client has a choice of responses to any situation and no longer has to operate on a default response programmed in childhood.

- **The archetypal trance**

In addition to symptomatic trances we also experience identity trances.[6] Frequently, we become so closely identified with a particular role that we create a trance identity. When this identity becomes our entire identity we lose touch with other aspects of ourselves. The identity becomes so ingrained that we respond out of it automatically; so focused on (entranced by) the identity that we no longer have access to other resources. Similarly, we fall under the spell of an archetypal trance. We can be so caught up in our role as a kind, caring person (Caregiver) that we lose access to the ability, or the need, to protect or defend ourselves (Warrior). A therapist can be entranced by the role of kind, caring, compassionate mother or sister that she forgets that she has the capacity in her Warrior archetype— to be firm and clear, set limits, and face what has to be done. Experiencing ourselves in only one role, be it victim (Orphan) or Caregiver (martyr), our ability to play other roles is temporarily unknown to us.

A word, a tone of voice, a glance, and even a thought can transport us from present time conscious awareness to an archetypal trance state of an earlier time. A promise can evoke the Innocent, a threat the Orphan and suddenly all other archetypal energies disappear from consciousness. The person who is ordinarily quite competent becomes, *in one area of her life,* a helpless child, dependent and/or abandoned. In the example above, whenever Ruth thought that Sam might leave and feared abandonment, she fell into the trance identity of the Innocent, and when I observed her pain I succumbed to the trance identity of the good Caregiver.

- **Breaking the trance**

There are many therapeutic activities that break trances, shed light on other resources, and enable clients to cope with the present situation in the present time instead of remaining limited to the meager coping responses of the past. Breaking a trance is similar to waking up. We ask clients to open their eyes, move their bodies, focus attention outside of themselves and come to full consciousness of the here and now, instead of the then and there.[7] To break an archetypal trance, in addition to waking the client and having her face the situation as it is today, we also activate other archetypes and give the client a new experience of coping so that the spells of the past no longer have power.

Back to Ruth:
Breaking the Therapist's Trance

First I needed to pay closer attention to what Ruth was doing and experiencing so I could meet her where she was and bring her awareness into the present time. I observed that whenever Ruth began to realize that Sam had left, she regressed to an emotional stage, or age, where she experienced her loss as a matter of life or death and said she wanted to die. Perhaps to defend against that pain she went into a future trance, just as she did as a child, and tells herself that it will be all right if she has faith and continues to do the right things. In this way Ruth enters the trance of the Innocent.[8]

However, Ruth was not the only one experiencing archetypal trance states. My Caregiver (mother) archetype was activated by Ruth's plight and until that moment in supervision, I had been unaware of it! I wanted to spare her suffering, to be supportive and nurturing, to answer her questions and help her understand— and none of this was helpful to her any longer. Techniques once essential in establishing our therapeutic relationship were no longer "age appropriate." My colleague in supervision had broken my trance when she asked me to open my eyes and become aware of what I was doing.

The Therapist's lesson

When we are aware of the arrival of the archetype— when we call on it or activate or awaken it— we can use the information and abilities it brings us. When we are not aware, when we are entranced, it uses us. I had been overprotective with Ruth and had not chosen my responses carefully; I had been unconscious of the significance of my relationship to her, and in that way I encouraged Ruth to stay in her dependent state.

My therapeutic tasks were to break our trances and teach Ruth to care for and stand up for herself — to develop autonomy instead of dependency. To accomplish these tasks I first had to break my own trance and take charge of the therapy instead of taking care of Ruth. Most important, I had to act on this, not merely talk to her about it.

I asked myself, "What is my role with this client? What are her goals? What are my goals? What developmental tasks does Ruth need to accomplish? How can I take charge of the therapy so that her best interests are considered? What therapeutic activities can get her where she needs to go?" I thought that I had "found" her, acknowledged her, and had even thought that we had agreed on her goals, but somehow I had taken her on to my path instead of preparing her to find her own.

Therapeutic activities: Establishing trust and autonomy

For the adult, trust and autonomy go hand in hand. The Innocent, however, has too much trust and not enough autonomy. Ruth needed to learn that she could trust herself, in that she could face the fall (Sam's leaving her) and survive. Ruth had to awaken her Warrior to ensure her autonomy and her internal Caregiver to soothe, reassure, and comfort herself.

I began to acknowledge Ruth and take charge of the therapy. My first step was to "find" her by describing her location and her emotions. "At times it seems like there's nothing to live for and at other times you have hopes that he will change" or "You are sad and hurt at what he has done but you are afraid to get angry for fear that would ruin your chances of getting him back." These were not interpretations but descriptions of her position. If I made interpretations she would argue with me.

I had made a major therapeutic mistake by implying that there might be a chance that Ruth and Sam would get back together. Once, when Ruth had asked if I thought there was ever a chance that they might get back together, I had replied in an offhand way, "I suppose that anything is possible." I said this as I might when talking to a friend in order to ease her pain or keep her hopes up. This, however, was not a social situation. In her literal trance state, Ruth had interpreted my words to mean that I thought that there was a chance they could work things out.

I needed to acknowledge this, so I said, "You are disappointed in me because you thought that I was telling you to continue to have hope that the relationship might someday work out." (I learned from this something that I should have learned before: never to answer a question when I didn't know the answer, and always to attend to the questions clients ask, and acknowledge the question itself before responding with an answer.)

Our relationship changed quickly when I concentrated on directing the dialogue back to Ruth and her own feelings, perceptions, and what was happening right then and there. Ruth was a thinker and logic dominated her life. She liked theoretical discussions of "why" and "tell me how." The "why's" and "tell me how's" were barriers to therapy; appeals to authority to tell her how it should be and to take care of her. Now that my own trance was broken, I was mindful and present in the therapy session and no longer answered these questions.

Therapy notes

A note to myself at this time:

I am replicating Sam's part in the relationship if I continue to allow her to stay outside of herself and in this "I have to understand it!" mode. This is a dead end and keeps us stuck. I can't fix her and I can't make her understand. Part of her task is to accept her own shadow, her own part in "devoting her life" with the expectation that she would get something back; her own damage that she did to herself by not getting out of a relationship in which she wasn't being treated well. I am not doing her any favors by not helping her to see this. If there has to be blame, if someone has to be right and the other wrong, we will continue this dance forever. It is my job to help her see this, it is not my job to make her feel better. I must keep her aware of what is happening in the present and keep myself in the present; I must be aware each minute in therapy of the process that is going on. I do not need to explain this to her. I am the one who needs to understand this. I can't make Ruth understand any more than she can make Sam understand. I have to change her experience of herself.

Also, I see that I have not given her a good model of behavior in that I didn't acknowledge my responsibility to take care of my own feelings and I continued to see her in therapy because I didn't want her to feel that I had given up on her! Now I have to change my approach and the assignment to take action may be a way to go about this.

Facing the fall

To break the trance of the shadow Innocent is to face the fall— the loss of innocence. Sam had left. It was over. Nothing Ruth could do would change that. He would take care of her no longer and it had nothing to do with whether or not she deserved to be taken care of or whether or not she was a good person. Ruth, however, needed concrete evidence of this and fortunately Sam soon provided it.

Sam— who had never explicitly told her that the marriage was over— filed for divorce. When Ruth received the papers she began her trance inducing activities, "I have to understand. People have to tell me. Why didn't he tell me? What did I do wrong? What does this other person have that I don't?" At one point she cried out, "People have to tell me. He has to tell me that he doesn't want a committed relationship!" I got her attention, asked her to look at me and replied, "Look at the papers, read what they say. He is telling you. The divorce papers are the message. The keys he asked you to return are the message!" Then, I attended to her but didn't comfort her. I acknowledged and affirmed her feelings and listened as she began to face the facts, and when she faced the facts she saw that her fantasy world was crumbling.

When Ruth was able to look back more objectively she saw that each time Sam had done something she didn't like, she had carefully explained to him what he had done wrong and believed that such explanations and scoldings would persuade him to change his behavior. When he lied to her, she would catch him up, become angry and self righteous, and demand that he never lie to her again. When he wouldn't make time for her she would complain and nag and talk to other people about how much she did for him and how little he did for her. Often, he ignored her when they were with others yet told her how special she was to him when they were alone. Her responses to all of this were to try to make him see that he was wrong and she was right and then sit back and wait for him to understand or agree with her. From her new vantage point she saw the futility of this.

Assignment in the here and now

I immediately assigned a series of practical tasks, things that she had to do differently to keep her from falling into the symptomatic trance and make her conscious of reality. I directed her to hire a lawyer, to begin the inventory of property and assets, and to tell her friends that they were divorcing.

Destination

Once both of our trances were broken Ruth made rapid progress. The assignment to take care of financial and property matters helped Ruth break the trance and face the fall. Quickly she saw that she had to care for herself. She allowed herself to feel her anger and used that anger to gather the strength she needed to fight for the property that was rightfully hers, to stop taking care of Sam, and to start taking care of herself. Although at first she tried to gather support for herself (and against Sam), she soon saw the futility of that and began to seek new friends and pursue new interests. Now that the spell was broken, Ruth could listen for her own call and pursue things she was genuinely interested in instead of centering her life on Sam's plans and Sam's interests. Ruth's turnabout was painful but amazingly quick and through it she learned that she could face pain and survive. My notes to myself from her last session read:

> I see a change in her from the Innocent/Orphan victim to a newer maturity. She says, "I hate to say this but I think all of this is a gift. I am being forced to see reality." She seems to be learning from each experience because she is awake to these experiences. She is taking action instead of relying on analysis; she is doing things that allow her to experience life instead defending against it. She hasn't solved all her problems but she isn't looking to others to solve them for her. More importantly, she embarks on the living of her own life with some enthusiasm. She no longer fits the personality disorder criteria, nor is she depressed. The fall of the Innocent has to be experienced. No one can describe it or tell you about the loss of the protection and hope for rescue; you have to be there yourself and no one on earth can do it for you.

Ruth's finding a life of her own paved the way for many of the other Innocents I've met in psychotherapy. I learned from Ruth the importance of the therapist-client relationship and I learned from Ruth to respect the strength of the Innocent who, once the trance is broken, blossoms into a complete person, ready to claim her own life; to survive and to prevail.

> **Working with Orphans...**
> **Preparing Mary for the Journey**
> Assessment: Low level orphan, orphaned from self
> Developmental tasks:
> > Learning to trust, learning to survive in the world
> > Learning to give and receive help
> Therapeutic tasks:
> > Awakening the Caregiver, Warrior and high level Orphan within
> Therapeutic activities:
> > Being trustworthy, setting limits
> Therapist lesson:
> > Finding myself in relation to the client instead of being politically correct

The Orphan and the Innocent are extremely sensitive to the feelings of others. One of the most serious effects of childhood trauma or traumatic parenting is that it can result in the victim orphaning herself. Orphans becomes numb, insensitive to their own feelings, and hypersensitive to the feelings of others. Innocents use their hypersensitivity to the feelings and needs of others to elicit care, protection, and nurturing. Orphans, on the other hand, use their hypersensitivity to become hyper-vigilant in order to protect themselves from further trauma. Each needs to become aware of and sensitive to her own emotions and learn to act to meet her own needs if she is to accomplish the developmental task of developing autonomy. Each must learn to act instead of react: to learn that she is capable of choosing how to respond; and to discover that she does not have to remain a victim forever.

Unlike the Innocent, the Orphan has experienced the fall. The Orphan knows she is on her own in the world and that there is no one to take care of her.[9] The ultimate gift of the Orphan is the recognition that even though we are alone— no mother or father to protect us— we don't have to do everything alone. The Orphan who comes to therapy, however, is usually a victim who lost her innocence far too soon and feels betrayed, powerless, cynical and angry. She has been traumatized, and in her interpersonal relations identifies herself completely in an Orphan mode. She has not yet claimed her gifts. Therapists have to take care not to make the mistake of seeing Orphans or victims only in the victim mode or Orphan mode. We must remember that every person is capable of taking a journey and finding her own "True North."

How not to be a politically correct therapist: Re-finding ourselves

In working with Ruth I learned that clients can put me in archetypal trances. It is easy to be over-protective of clients who have been sexually abused or treated badly and natural to want to take care of them. Before we know it we are "walking on egg shells," fearful that we will reactivate their fears and mistrust. The therapist who has been sexually abused is in danger of identifying with her client and fighting the battles a client must learn to fight for herself.

At the other extreme, the therapist who has never acknowledged her own woundedness and doesn't understand why the victim can't just "get on with it," cannot meet the client where she is and often tries to be too directive with the client. When we find ourselves in either place— identifying with or struggling with a client— we must get supervisory help. However, we have to be careful about, not only our own prejudices and blind spots, but also those of our supervisors. Sometimes supervisors have agendas, too.

Learning another lesson with Mary the Orphan

Mary, whom we first met in earlier chapters, was a victim of childhood sexual abuse. At the time she revealed this to me, the therapeutic community had only recently begun to realize the extent of the impact of childhood sexual abuse. Until that time, the subject had seldom been broached in training programs for therapists, and few had studied the effects of abuse on children or the efficacy of treatment methods. Now, books and workshops appeared daily on the scene containing all the latest advice on how to treat adult victims of childhood abuse. Suddenly, there were experts everywhere who knew the "right way" to treat victims. We were told that there were things you should and should not say to victims. Therapists were advised to believe everything the client said, and the popular books our clients read told them, "If you think you were abused, you probably were." Sympathetic therapists soon became advocates who accompanied clients to court, advised confrontations with perpetrators, told adults to cut off all communication with their families, and settled in to long courses of therapy in which the victim was required to re-live the victimization in order to recover from the trauma. All victims were to be treated alike.

During and immediately after my training as a therapist I had worked in one of the first programs dedicated to treating all family members in cases of family sexual abuse. Subsequently, I also worked in early correctional programs for sex offenders. I had seen the many different ways that abuse could affect victims, and hesitated at first to follow what seemed to me to be the party line or politically correct policy instead of an individual policy for each victim. However, I felt pressure at workshops and in group supervision when others made statements like, "You can't say that to a victim," or when they implied that we had to excuse a victim's bad behavior because they had been abused. Now I encountered therapists who encouraged female victims to hate and distrust all men, and therapists who did not treat mature women as adults but rather as children who needed to have someone compensate for their horrible childhood. For a while I once again paid more attention to the "experts" than I did to my own experience and followed the body of thought that said that all victims had to be treated a certain way and that therapists who deviated from the party line were not behaving properly. Again I felt a discordance between what I was advised to do and what my own experience had taught me. When I became aware of the hero's journey model I decided to re-evaluate what I was doing in therapy with Mary. The first step was to find myself in relation to her.

You will recall that Mary didn't tell me at first that she had been sexually abused. Her experience with two of her former therapists had made her wary. One therapist told her that he had never worked with anyone who had been sexually abused and, therefore, didn't believe her. Her next therapist insisted that she confront her abuser and later dismissed her from therapy when she didn't "behave" appropriately. For that reason, Mary was suspicious of me and I now realized that her suspicions alerted my Warrior, not my Caregiver. For a long time I couldn't allow myself to get close enough to her to see the world through her eyes because I felt it necessary to protect myself. Mary, far more attuned to my feelings than to her own, sensed my wariness and told me only what she wanted me to hear.

- **Establishing Trust**

The wound of abuse and trauma in her early life had precipitated Mary's Fall. She had never been prepared for the journey and at this point was trying to survive in the only way she knew how— by constantly demanding that others care for her and not abandon her and doing so in such a way that even the best intentioned helpers could not give her what she asked.

I realized that Mary, like Ruth, was trying to get others to take care of her and doing it in the same way that she had done all of her life. What had worked in the past to protect Mary— being vigilant, distrustful, demanding then withdrawing, threatening suicide, daring others to take her on and proving that they couldn't do it— was no longer working. However, these tactics attracted attention and proved her personal theories about the unreliability of others.

In order for me to help Mary accomplish the developmental tasks of surviving and learning to relate to the outside world I needed to be trustworthy and present in our relationship in. Once again, I had to assume a parental role, but I could not be an indulgent parent, I needed to teach her how to interact with the outside world so that she could give and receive help in an appropriate way.

- **Relationship of therapist to client**

We keep clients in a victim mode when we continue to do things for them that they are capable of doing themselves. No one can make up to anyone else for the childhood she didn't have. All we can do is find them, respect them, and teach them to do the things they haven't yet learned to do.

Mary's childhood had been brutal, but instead of activating my sympathetic Caregiver, Mary had activated my Warrior when I felt the need to protect myself from her. When I became aware of this, I became conscious of the need to enlist my Warrior energy to set my own limits and teach Mary to protect and defend herself.

At this point Mary needed to accomplish three developmental tasks:

1. Learning to trust in her own ability to take care of and protect herself (stop being a victim) by becoming a Warrior on her own behalf instead of a remaining a victim.

2. Learning to survive in the world: to take responsibility for her own actions and her own emotions (becoming a Caregiver to herself), and

3. Learning to relate to others as a peer (rising to the highest levels of the Orphan).

People in the preparation phase of the journey need assignments they can carry out in the real world. They may have correctly analyzed the origins of their problems, but until they experience themselves differently, they are not ready to move on. Taking direct action is a primary coping skill. Therefore, I began a series of what I call assignments in the real world. These are assignments that have a function in the therapy, keep the client doing psychological work between sessions, and also have a meaningful function in their own lives.(Mary's assignment to stand up for herself with Olivia as described earlier is one example.) The purpose of these assignments is to change clients' inner experience of themselves and, in O'Hanlon's words, change their "doing" of the problem and of their lives. Assignments make the client experience doing something different in the world they live in today, as opposed to the restricted world of her childhood. This is another way of facing dragons, breaking the trance and opening up resources and possibilities.

In the end, there were three different types of therapeutic activities that helped Mary develop her higher level Orphan, Innocent, Caregiver and Warrior. These were: assignments in the here and now to learn autonomy and self reliance (learning to take responsibility for own actions), participation in group therapy to learn the basic caregiver skills instead of being a martyr and giving only to others (described in an earlier chapter), and also participation in the group to learn to take responsibility for her own emotions (becoming aware of her own emotions and learning that only she could do something about what was bothering her).

- **Therapeutic activities:**

  Being in the body — Orphans and Innocents who have experienced physical trauma, are as dissociated from their bodily sensations as they are from their emotions. Adults who have not learned emotional survival skills frequently have few physical survival skills. They may neglect good health practices, have poor eating habits, get little or no exercise, or neglect their physical surroundings. A good metaphor for trust in self and autonomy is learning to swim. Others can teach you and tell you how to swim but no one can swim for you. If you are drowning and try to fight the rescuer, you both drown. Until you learn to swim you can at least learn to cooperate with the rescuer.

  Mary had never been taught to swim when she was a child. Therefore, I asked her to sign up for lessons at the local Y. Undertaking this assignment took enormous courage on Mary's part. It is difficult for adults to face the fear of the water, to be seen in public in a bathing suit, to trust the instructor to take care of them, and to trust the water to hold them up. Learning to swim— to prove to herself that she was capable of saving her own life— was an incredible victory for Mary. At one point she thought about quitting because she was the slowest swimmer in her class. I reminded her that if she fell out of a boat in the middle of the lake there would be no one there to compete with her for fastest time to the shore. I also reminded her that swimming isn't about how fast anyone else can swim but about how you can keep your head above water and not panic. The metaphors about swimming, life lines, and rescue were not lost on Mary, and in the course of carrying out this assignment she learned that she could play an active part in saving her own life.

When we break the trance of the Innocent or Orphan, or break the therapist's trance of the Caregiver or the Warrior, we gain access to all of the resources of therapist and client alike. When I consider clients like Ruth and Mary as Innocents and Orphans, I can help them accomplish the essential developmental tasks that awaken other archetypes and send them on their journeys. When I also attend to the archetypes my clients awaken in me I am better able to perform my job as a therapist than I was when I thought of my clients in terms of symptoms, labels or diagnostic categories. *Labels and diagnoses make us think of our differences. Archetypes help us think of our similarities.*

For Ruth and Mary the essential work of preparation for the journey has been accomplished. The therapy is over but the journey continues. Having solved the problems of the ego, they can now, if they choose, face the mysteries of the soul. They face forward, ready to find their own paths.

Summary

I end where I began. I continue to ask myself the same questions. I ask if I am a protector or the one urging a client to take risks? Can I tell my client when I am lost, or not? Can I tell my client how I feel or must I make note of how I feel and stay focused on my client's feelings? Are there times when a client's feelings are irrelevant? Should I encourage a client to go deeper into the crevice of a symptom or to pull back from the edge? The continuing questions I ask are, "Who am I?" and "Who is the client?" and "Where am I?" and "Where is the client?" and "Where are we trying to go?" and then, "How can I use my abilities, feelings, sensations and my knowledge of the territory to help my client get there?" I'm still asking the questions but now I answer myself based on the needs of the client and not what an expert tells me I should do. I continue to fight my dragons.

I've used the guide and journey metaphor because it is useful and efficient. It allows me to consider a context comprehensive enough to include the medical model but also to consider Jungian, developmental, existential/humanist, family therapy and competency-based, solution-oriented brief therapies. It is important to me however, to use this model as a map for myself and not as a theory to teach to clients. We can't waste valuable time teaching theory; we have to use the limited time we have to do therapy.

Permissions

The author gratefully acknowledges permission from these sources to reprint the following:

Excerpt from the poem *This Time,* from *Fire in the Earth,* copyright ©1992 by David Whyte, reprinted by permission of Many Rivers Company, PO Box 868, Langley, WA 98260

Six Steps for Adult Children of Dysfunctional Theories from *The Handout Book* copyright © 1995 by Bill O'Hanlon, reprinted by permission of Bill O'Hanlon.

Extended quotations from *The Hero Within: Six Archetypes We Live By,* copyright ©1986, 1989, 1998 by Carol S. Pearson, reprinted by permission of HarperCollins Publishers, Inc.

Extensive quotations from *Awakening the Heroes Within: Twelve Archetypes to Help Us Find Ourselves and Transform Our World,* copyright ©1991 by Carol S. Pearson, reprinted by permission of HarperCollins Publishers, Inc.

End Notes

Preface

1. Carol S. Pearson, *Awakening the Heroes Within: Twelve Archetypes to Help us Find Ourselves and Transform our World* (San Francisco: Harper Collins, 1991).

Introduction

1. Michael P. Nichols, *The Self in the System: Expanding the Limits of Family Therapy* (New York: Brunner/Mazel (1987), p.235.

2. American Psychiatric Association (Eds.) *Diagnostic and Statistical Manual of Mental Disorders* (4th ed.) (Washington, DC: American Psychiatric Association, 1994).

Chapter One

1. Michael White and David Epston, in *Narrative Means to Therapeutic Ends* (New York: W. W. Norton & Company. Inc., 1990) present a different approach from that of the biological and physical sciences that seek causes and pathology.

2. Betty Freidan, *The Fountain of Age* (New York: Simon & Schuster, 1993). Children are potential heroes but as they are neither free to choose nor in a legal community of equals, they can not yet begin the journey. However, we can be aware, as parents, teachers and therapists that it is our responsibility to prepare them for the journey.

3. The concept of soul used here differs from the religious connotation of the word soul and relates to the original meaning of the word "psyche."

4. Erik H. Erikson, *Childhood and Society* (2nd ed.) (New York: W. W. Norton & Company, Inc. 1963).

5. Carol S. Pearson, *The Hero Within: Six Archetypes We Live By* (San Francisco: Harper & Row 1986), p.xxi.

6. Erik H. Erikson, *Childhood and Society* (2nd ed.) (New York: W. W. Norton & Company, Inc. 1963).

7. Robert A. Johnson, *Inner work: Using Dreams and Active Imagination for Personal Growth* (San Francisco: Harper Row, 1986), p. 22.

8. Anthony Stevens, *Archetypes: A Natural History of the Self* (New York: William Morrow and Company, Inc. 1982), p.16.

9. Carol S. Pearson, *Awakening the Heroes Within: Twelve Archetypes to Help us Find Ourselves and Transform our World* (San Francisco: Harper Collins,1991). This is an essential reference for those interested in applied archetypal psychology.

10. "Because the guides are truly archetypal, and hence reside as energy within the unconscious psychological life of all people everywhere, they exist both inside and outside the individual human soul. They live in us, but even more importantly,

we live in them. We can find them by going inward (to our own dreams, fantasies, and often actions as well) or by going outward (to myth, legend, art, literature, and religion, and, as pagan cultures often did, to the constellations of the sky and the birds and animals of the earth). Thus they provide images of the hero within and beyond ourselves" Carol S. Pearson, *Awakening the Heroes Within, p. 6.*

11. The descriptions of the archetypes are adapted from Carol S. Pearson, *Awakening the Heroes Within.*

12. Joseph Campbell, Mythological Themes in Creative Literature and Art. In Joseph Campbell (Ed.), *Myths, Dreams, and Religion* (Dallas, TX Spring Publications, Inc. 1970), p. 141.

13. My purpose here is not to fit all of Erikson's stages into Pearson's theory but to describe a way to practice psychotherapy that has theoretical relevance and that works. Therefore, I have concentrated on the essential stages of trust and autonomy and have not addressed Erikson's stages of initiative and industry directly.

14. William J. Doherty, *SoulSearching: Why Psychology Must Promote Moral Responsibility* (New York: Basic Books, *1995).*

Chapter Two

1. Carol S. Pearson, *Awakening the Heroes Within:*

Twelve Archetypes to Help us Find Ourselves and Transform our World (San Francisco: HarperCollins, *1991*), *p. 91.*

2. Carol S. Pearson, *Awakening the Heroes Within, p. 71.*

3. Carol S. Pearson, *Awakening the Heroes Within, p. 84.*

4. Carol S. Pearson, *Awakening the Heroes Within,* p.109

5. Carol S. Pearson, *The Hero Within: Six Archetypes We Live By (San* Francisco: Harper & Row 1986), *p. 1.*

6. David Whyte, Self Portrait in *Fire in the Earth* (Langley, Washington: Many Rivers Press, 1992).

7. Joseph Campbell and William Moyers, *The Power of Myth* (New York: Doubleday, 1988).

8. Carol S. Pearson, *Awakening the Heroes Within, p. 95.*

9. Sheldon Kopp, *All God's Children Are Lost, But Only a Few Can Play the Piano* (New York: Prentice Hall Press, 1991).

10. Thomas Moore, *Care of the Soul* (New York: HarperCollins, 1992)

11. Anthony Stevens, *Private Myths: Dreams and Dreaming* (Cambridge, Mass: Harvard University Press, 1995).

12. David Whyte, *National Public Radio, Fresh air with Terry Gross* [Cassette Recording]. (Princeton, New Jersey: Spencer Entertainment Enterprise, 1994).

13. Joyce M. Hawkins (Ed.), *The Oxford Reference Dictionary* (New York: Oxford University Press,1986).

14. Joseph Campbell, *The Hero with a Thousand Faces*. (2nd ed.) (Princeton, NJ: Bollingen Series,1968), p. 51.

15. Carol S. Pearson, *Awakening the Heroes Within*, *p.*123.

16. Carol S. Pearson, *Awakening the Heroes Within*, *p.*148.

17. David Whyte, This Time, in *Fire in the Earth*, p. 25.

18. Carol S. Pearson, *Awakening the Heroes Within*, *p.*165.

19. Robert A. Johnson, *Inner work: Using Dreams and Active Imagination for Personal Growth* (San Francisco: Harper Row, 1986), p. 22.

20. Robert Fritz, *The Path qf Least Resistance: Learning to be the Creative Force in Your Own Life* (2nd ed.) (New York: Fawcett Columbine, 1989).

21. Carol S. Pearson, *Awakening the Heroes Within*, *p.* 137.

22. Michael J. Mahony, *Human Change Process: The Scientific Foundation of Psychotherapy.* (New York: Basic Books, 1991), p.4.

23. Carol S. Pearson, *Awakening the Heroes Within,* p. 184.

24. Carol S. Pearson, *Awakening the Heroes Within,* p. 209.

25. Richard Simon. From the editor. *The Family Therapy Networker, (21* July/August 1997), p. 2.

26. Angeles Arrien,*The Four-Fold Way: Walking the Paths of the Warrior, Teacher, Healer, and Visionary (San* Francisco: Harper San Francisco, 1993).

27. Carol S. Pearson, *Awakening the Heroes Within,* p.193.

28. Rollo May, Psychotherapy and the Daimonic. In Joseph Campbell (Ed.), *Myths, dreams, and religion* (2nd ed.) (Dallas, Texas: Spring Publications, Inc. 1988), p. 209.

29. Rollo May, *Psychotherapy and the Daimonic.*

30. Michael J. Mahony, *Human Change Process, p. xi*

31. Carol S. Pearson, *Awakening the Heroes Within,* p. 220.

32. Bill O'Hanlon, *The Handout Book (*Omaha: Possibility Press, 1996), p. 157.

33. Tom Wilson, *Never Get Too Personally Involved with Your Own Life* (New York: Sheed and Ward, Inc. 1975).

Questions to lead you on a self guided voyage

I   " An articulated, an all- worked- out psychology is better spoken of as a theology or a philosophy or a movement, and the activity performed in its name and called "therapy" (Freudian, Jungian, Rogerian, Reichean) is more truly indoctrination or conversion. It is more likely to be ideology than psychologizing. Perhaps there can be no discipline of therapeutic psychology, only an activity of psychotherapy."
James Hillman, *Re-visioning Psychology* (2d ed.) (New York: Harper Collins, 1992), p. 145.

Chapter Three

1. Irvin D.Yolam, *Existential Psychotherapy (*New York: Basic Books, Inc. 1980), p. 410

2. It is especially important to rule out Bi-Polar disorders which are sometimes difficult to diagnose until you have observed the client over a longer period of time.

3. Leston Havens, *Making Contact: Uses of Language in Psychotherapy (Cambridge:* Harvard University Press 1986), p. 16.

4. Leston Havens, *Making Contact, p. 28.*

5. Note: this is not meant as an interpretation. If I had not accurately reflected her feelings this statement could have been misunderstood and become a barrier between us.

6. James Hillman calls this the parental fallacy and says that working through this fallacy is difficult because it is not a "mere logical error or displaced concreteness, or a difficult step in a therapeutic process toward individual self determination. Working through the parental fallacy is more like a religious conversion-out of our secularism, out of personalism, out of our monotheism, develop mental-ism and belief in causality." James Hillman, *The Soul's Code: In Search of Character and Calling* (New York: Random House, 1996), p. 90. 1 do not go quite so far as Hillman but agree that we need not always assume that poor parenting is always correlated with poor outcomes for the child.

7. Bill O'Hanlon and Sandy Beadle, *A Field Guide to PossibilityLand- Possibility Therapy Methods (Omaha:* Possibility Press, 1994), p.15.

8. Yvonne M. Dolan, *Resolving Sexual Abuse: Solution Focused Therapy and Ericksonian Hypnosis for Adult Survivors* (New York: W. W. Norton & Company, Inc. 1991).

9. Bill O'Hanlon, *The Handout Book(* Omaha: Possibility Press, 1996), and Bill O'Hanlon and Sandy Beadle, *A Field Guide to PossibilityLand.*

Chapter Four

1. Anthony Storr, *The Art of Psychotherapy* (2nd ed.) (New York: Routledge, 1990), p. 84.

2. Bill O'Hanlon, *The Handout Book (Omaha:* Possibility Press, 1996).

3. Bill O'Hanlon, *The Handout Book.*

4. Yvonne Dolan presents a way to do this when working with victims of sexual abuse. She first listens to her clients' story of the abuse (acknowledgment) then proceeds with a solution focused approach in which she uses a first session question about what has changed since the person made the appointment, a solution focused recovery scale, the miracle question, a first session formula task, and an assignment to talk to an older, wiser self." Yvonne M. Dolan, *Resolving Sexual Abuse: Solution Focused Therapy and Ericksonian Hypnosis for Adult Survivors* (New York: W. W. Norton & Company, Inc. 1991).

5. Steve de Shazer, What is it about Brief Therapy that Works? In Jeffrey K. Zweig and Stephen G. Gilligan (Eds.), *Brief Therapy: Myths, Metaphors and Methods(* New York: Brunner/Mazel, 1990), p. 492.

6. Bill O'Hanlon asks clients how they 'do' depression, or multiple personality disorder, or 'co-dependency' and thereby creates action correlates for feelings, or disorders and separates the problem from the person. Bill O'Hanlon, *The Handout Book (Omaha:* Possibility Press, 1996), p. 9.

7. Donald Meichenbaum and Dennis Turk, *Facilitating Treatment Adherence: A Practitioner's Guidebook (*New York: Plenum Press, 1987).

Chapter Five

1. James Hillman, *Re-visioning Psychology* (2nd ed.) (New York: Harper Collins, 1992), p. 145.

2. When designing a house for a client and architect has to adhere to certain standards, know about structure, the suitability of materials, regulations: building codes. The architect is hired by clients because he or she has knowledge they don't have. However, within the structure of that knowledge there is room for creativity in the collaborative effort of the architect and client to create some thing unique that meets the client's needs and desires. Similarly, the therapist and the client can collaborate in a relationship that meets the clients' needs and wants, and violates the integrity of neither.

3. Children are good hypnotic subjects and children also use self induced trances to cope with experiences they can't integrate or tolerate. They will, for example, dissociate from sexual abuse or develop amnesia for many types of types of trauma. The coping mechanism that served a child well in child hood becomes a symptom when it is the *only* way that person can cope as an adult. Steve Wolinsky calls this a bad trance. Once the trance is broken the client has a choice of responses to any situation, he or she no longer has to operate on the default response programed in childhood. Stephen Wolinsky, *Trances People Live: Healing Approaches in Quantum Psychology,* (Falls Village, CT: The Bramble Company, 1991).

4. I distinguish between a reason and an excuse. Mary's childhood was the reason she hadn't learned. Once she realized this and recognized what she had to learn, she could no longer us her childhood as an excuse.

5. To learn more about handling anger and assertiveness without ending a relationship see Harriet Lerner, *the Dance of Anger* (New York: Harper and Row, 1985).

6. This is not to say that these techniques can't be used in any phase of the journey. However, they are particularly effective here.

7. Michael White and David Epston, *Narrative Means to Therapeutic Ends* (New York: W. W. Norton & Company. Inc., 1990).

8. Albert Ellis and W. Dryden, *The Practice of Rational-Emotive Therapy* (*Secaucus,* NJ: Lyle Stuart, 1987).

9. David D. Bums, *Feeling Good: The New Mood Therapy* (New York: Signet, 1980).

10. Stephen Wolinsky, *Trances People Live: Healing Approaches in Quantum Psychology* (Falls Village, CT: The Bramble Company, 1991).

11. Bill O' Hanlon and Sandy Beadle, A *Field Guide to PossibilityLand, p. 85*

Chapter Six

1. Robert Buckman, M.D., *How to Break Bad News: A Guide for Health Care Professionals* (Baltimore, MD: John Hopkins University Press, 1992), p. 63.

2. James Hillman, *Re-visioning Psychology* (2nd ed.) (New York: HarperCollins, 1992), p. 83.

3. Steven Bierman, in an article on medical hypnosis in the journal *Advances,* contends that the attribution of authority "...is an inevitable consequence of mammalian child-rearing. If the species is to survive, the elders must instruct the young. Like all patterns in mental life, the pattern of authority can be readily resuscitated and utilized. One need only create and experience a reminiscent state of dependency (for example through a threatening illness, or in a hypnotic trance), and the pattern of authority revives with tremendous power." Steven F. Bierman, Medical Hypnosis. *Advances: The Journal of Mind-Body Health, 11* (1995), pp. 69-71.

4. Charles Hampton-Turner, Maps *of the Mind* (New York: MacMillan Publishing Co. 1982).

5. Irvin D.Yolam, *Existential Psychotherapy (*New York: Basic Books, Inc. 1980), p. 405.

6. It isn't necessary to ponder whether Freud or Yalom is right, but merely to ask the question Carl Rogers asked after years of thought on this subject. "... in my early professional years I was

asking the question, 'How can I treat, or cure, or change this person? Now I would phrase the question in this way: How can I provide a relationship which this person may use for his own personal growth?'" Carl R. Rogers, *On Becoming a Person* (Boston: Houghton Mifflin Company, 1961), p. 32.

7. William Doherty argues persuasively that with the disintegration of the moral center of our society, therapists' primary focus is no longer to liberate people from the constrictions of a repressive society, but that we now must take a new look at our role in the larger society and consider social responsibility as well as individual freedom and well being. William J. Doherty, *SoulSearching: Why Psychology Must Promote Moral Responsibility* (New York: Basic Books, 1995).

8. Bill O'Hanlon, *The Handout Book (Omaha:* Possibility Press, 1996), p.26.

9. Lacklon Forrow, Preventive Ethics: Expanding the Horizons of Clinical Ethics. *Journal of Clinical Ethics.* 4 (4): 287-294, 1993 Winter.

10. Anthony Stevens, *Private Myths: Dreams and Dreaming* (Cambridge, Massachusetts: Harvard University Press, 1995).

Chapter Seven

1. Bill O'Hanlon and Sandy Beadle, *A Field Guide to PossibilityLand: Possibility Therapy Methods* (Omaha: Possibility Press, 1994).

2. Louis Breger, *From Instinct to Identity* (Englewood Cliffs, NJ: Prentice Hall, Inc. 1974).

3. Steven F. Bierman, Medical Hypnosis. *Advances: The Journal of Mind-Body Health, 11* (1995), pp. 69-71.

4. Trance phenomena are negative and positive hallucination, different sensations such as numbness and lack of pain, amnesia and hypermnesia, age regression and progression, expansion and contraction of time, association and dissociation, and various physical sensations such as feeling heat or cold, arm levitation, catalepsy, and increase or decrease in blood rate and flow. Bill O'Hanlon, *The Handout Book,* (Omaha: Possibility Press, 1996),

5. Stephen Wolinsky, *Trances People Live: Healing Approaches in Quantum Psychology* (Falls Village, CT: The Bramble Company, 1991), p.7

6. Stephen Wolinsky, *Trances People Live.*

7. Wolinsky has written several books describing his method of breaking the trance, and they are a useful addition to any therapeutic repertoire. There are also special techniques to use when clients have experienced severe trauma and need to re-experience the trauma in a safe situation. Yvonne Dolan uses symbols of the present to help keep clients aware that they are now adults and don't have to respond in the habitual ways of their childhood . Stephen Wolinsky, *Trances People Live: Healing Approaches in Quantum Psychology* (Falls Village, CT: The Bramble Company, 1991). Yvonne M. Dolan, *Resolving Sexual Abuse: Solution Focused Therapy and Ericksonian Hypnosis for Adult Survivors* (New York: W. W. Norton & Company, Inc. 1991). Stephen Wolinsky, *The Dark Side of*

the Inner Child (Norfolk, CT: Bramble Books, 1993).

8. Pearson says that the shadow side of innocence refuses the fall. That, not wanting to see that someone can't be trusted, she "keeps walking intothe same abusive situations and getting battered and mistreated time and time again ... People who remain in the initial mode of innocence may pretend to be indepen dent, but underneath, they expect institutions, employers, friends, and spouses to take care of them. They rarely carry their own share of responsibility although they are 'very good' and may work hard. Others often do love and instinctively care for them as we do for little children. So in this way the Innocents' lives often work — at least until they lose their job or their spouse, or their friends and colleagues stop taking care of them and expect them to grow up... They assume that others want what they want because they often do not see the other person as real and separate." Carol S. Pearson, *Awakening the Heroes Within: Twelve Archetypes to Help Us Find Ourselves and Transform our World* (San Francisco: HarperCollins, 1991), p.78.

9. I use the feminine pronoun because most of the Orphans I have seen in therapy are women who were victimized as children. However, men are Orphans and Innocents, too. Each of us has an Orphan archetype. There is nothing pathological about being an Orphan; but when the Orphan archetype is the only archetype activated, you are limited in your ability to live your own life and are condemned to live a life that others have chosen for you.

References

Arrien, A. (1993). *The four-fold way.* San Francisco: HarperSanFrancisco.

American Psychiatric Association (Eds.). (1994). *Diagnostic and statistical manual of mental disorders (4th ed.).* Washington, D.C.: American Psychiatric Association.

Bierman, S. F. (1995). *Medical Hypnosis.* Advances: The Journal of Mind-Body Health, 11. pp. 69-71.

Buckman, R., M.D. (1992). *How to break bad news: A guide for health care professionals.* Baltimore, MD: Johns Hopkins University Press.

Burns, D., D. (1980). *Feeling good: The new mood therapy.* New York: Signet.

Campbell, J. (1968). *The hero with a thousand faces.* (2nd ed.). Princeton, NJ: Bollingen Series.

Campbell, J. (1970). *Mythological themes in creative literature and art.* In J. Campbell (Ed.), *Myths, dreams and religion* (pp. 138-175). Dallas, TX: Spring Publications, Inc.

Campbell, J., & Moyers, B. (1988). *The power of myth.* New York: Doubleday.

Corey, G. (1991). *Theory and practice of counseling and psychotherapy.* (4th ed.) Pacific Grove, CA: Brooks /Cole Publishing Company.

Csikszentmihalyi, M. (1993). *The evolving self: a psychology for the third millenium.* New York: HarperCollins.

de Shazer, S. (1990). *What is it about brief therapy that works?* In J. K. Zeig & S. G. Gilligan (Eds.), *Brief therapy: Myths, metaphors and methods* (pp. 492). New York: Brunner/Mazel.

Doherty, W. J. (1995). *Soul searching: Why psychology must promote moral responsibility.* New York: Basic Books.

Dolan, Y. M. (1991). *Resolving sexual abuse: solution-focused therapy and Ericksonian hypnosis for adult survivors.* New York: W.W. Norton & Company, Inc.

Ellis, A., & Dryden, W. (1987). *The practice of rational-emotive therapy.* Secaucus, NJ: Lyle Stuart.

Erikson, E. H. (1963). *Childhood and society.* (2nd ed.). New York: W.W. Norton & Company, Inc.

Freidan, B. (1993). *The fountain of age.* New York: Simon & Schuster.

Fritz, R. (1989). *The path of least resistance: Learning to be the creative force in your own life.* (2nd ed.). New York: Fawcett Columbine.

Hampton-Turner, C. (1982). *Maps of the Mind.* New York: MacMillan Publishing Co., Inc.

Havens, L. (1986). *Making contact: Uses of language in psychotherapy.* Cambridge: Harvard University Press.

Hawkins, J. M. (Ed.). (1986). *The Oxford reference dictionary.* New York: Oxford University Press.

Hillman, J. (1978). *The myth of analysis: Three essays in archetypal psychology.* New York: HarperCollins.

Hillman, J. (1992). *Re-visioning psychology.* (2nd ed.). New York: HarperCollins.

Hillman, J. (1996). *The soul's code: In search of character and calling.* New York: Random House.

Johnson, R. A. (1986). *Inner work: Using dreams and*

active imagination for personal growth. San Francisco: Harper & Row.
Jung, C. G. (1963). *Memories, dreams and reflections.* New York: Pantheon Books.
Kopp, S. (1972). *If you meet the Buddha on the road, kill him! The pilgrimage of psychotherapy patients.* Palo Alto, CA: Science and Behavior Books.
Kopp, S. (1991). *All God's children are lost, but only a few can play the piano: Finding a life that is truly your own.* New York: Prentice Hall Press.
Lerner, H. G. (1985). *The dance of anger.* New York: Harper and Row.
May, R. (1988). *Psychotherapy and the daimonic.* In J. Campbell (Ed.), *Myths, dreams, and religion* (2nd ed., pp. 196-210). Dallas, Texas: Spring Publications, Inc.
Meichenbaum, D., & Turk, D. C. (1987). *Facilitating treatment adherence: A practitioner's guide book.* New York: Plenum Press.
Moore, T. (1992) *Care of the soul.* New York: HarperCollins.
Nichols, M. P. (1987). *The self in the system: Expanding the limits of family therapy.* New York: Brunner/Mazel.
O'Hanlon, B. (1996). *The handout book.* Omaha: Possibility Press.
O'Hanlon, B., & Beadle, S. (1994). *A field guide to possibilityland: Possibility therapy methods.* Omaha: Possibility Press.
Oliver, M. (1986). *Dream work.* New York: Atlantic Monthly Press.
Pearson, C. S. (1986). *The hero within: Six archetypes we live by.* San Francisco: Harper & Row.

Pearson, C. S. (1991). *Awakening the heroes within: Twelve archetypes to help us find ourselves and transform our world.* San Francisco: HarperCollins.

Rico, G. L. (1991). *Pain and Possibility: Writing your way through personal crisis.* Los Angelos: Jeremy P. Tarcher, Inc.

Rogers, C. R. (1961). *On becoming a person.* Boston: Houghton Mifflin Company.

Simon, R. (1997). *From the editor.* The Family Therapy Networker, 21(July/August), 2.

Sinetar, M. (1987). *Do what you love, the money will follow: Discovering your right livelihood.* New York: Dell Publishing.

Stevens, A. (1982). *Archetypes: A natural history of the self.* New York: William Morrow and Company, Inc.

Stevens, A. (1995). *Private myths: Dreams and dreaming.* Cambridge, Massachusetts: Harvard University Press.

Storr, A. (1973). *Jung.* Glasgow, Scotland: William Collins & Co. Ltd.

Storr, A. (1990). *The art of psychotherapy.* (2nd ed.). New York: Routledge.

Watzlawick, P. (1990). *Therapy is what you say it is.* In J. K. Zeig & S. G. Gilligan (Eds.), *Brief therapy: Myths, methods and metaphors* (pp. 492). New York: Bruner/Mazel.

White, M., & Epston, D. (1990). *Narrative means to therapeutic ends. New York: W.W. Norton & Company, Inc.*

Whyte, D. (1992). *Fire in the earth.* Langley, WA: Many Rivers Press.

Whyte, D. (1994). National Public Radio, *Fresh air with Terry Gross* [Cassette Recording]. Princeton,

New Jersey: Spencer Entertainment Enterprise.
Wilson, T. (1975). *Never get too personally involved with your own life.* New York: Sheed and Ward, Inc.
Wolinsky, S. (1991). *Trances people live: Healing approaches in quantum psychology.* Falls Village, CT: The Bramble Company.
Yalom, I. D. (1980). *Existential psychotherapy.* New York: Basic Books, Inc.

About the Author

Patricia R. Adson, Ph.D., LP is a licensed psychologist, psychotherapist, and teacher in Rochester, Minnesota, where she has a private practice as a psychotherapist and teaches graduate courses in psychology and counseling at St. Mary's University in Minnesota. In addition, she conducts training workshops in Minnesota and Washington, D.C.. She is also the author of *A Princess and Her Garden: A Fable of Awakening and Arrival,* Lone Oak Press Ltd., Red Wing MN 55066.

Other Books and Materials from Type & Temperament, Inc. / Type & Archetype Press—

BOOKS

Invisible Forces I— Understanding the Archetypes in Your Family System, by Carol S. Pearson, Ph.D.
This was developed as a workbook to accompany Pearson's bestselling *"Awakening the Heroes Within— 12 Archetypes."* But it is also a workbook designed for the practical application of *Awakening the Heroes Within* concepts, to family systems— both your present family, and your family of origin, as measured by the Family Systems Index™ developed by Pearson.

Invisible Forces II—Harnessing the Power of Archetypes to Improve Your Career & Workplace, by Carol S. Pearson, Ph.D.
The definitive book on archetypes and the workplace, this was also designed as a workbook to accompany Pearson's *"Awakening the Heroes Within."* But is is a powerful stand-alone work, with charts and summaries that give an excellent overview of the archetypes and how they present themselves in our working lives. Useful with Pearson's organizational Culture Index,™ Team Culture Index,™ and Individual Performance Index.™

Introduction to Archetypes, by Carol S. Pearson, Ph.D.
A booklet to give workshop participants and others a general overview of archetypes and the 12 Pearsonian archetypes, and how they can be applied in relationships and workplace settings.

Give Yourself the Unfair Advantage, by Wm. D. G. Murray.
The *"most appealing of all the books that are out there on the Myers-Briggs Type Indicator®,"* according to *What Color is Your Parachute.* Delightful Ashleigh Brilliant "Pot-Shots®" (cartoon/ epigrams) illustrate each point, each followed by a serious lesson on Type. Result is a book that gets read and remembered, generates enthusiasm, and gets folks telling their friends and family about the concepts of type that changed their lives for the better.

And You Didn't Think You Had a Prayer, by Wm. D. G. Murray.
Sixteen serious prayers for the 16 Types. Memorable, insightful, these will speak to you. There's one for you, and each of your friends and family. *A reader said, "You have touched my very soul. I'm giving this to all my friends."*

When ENFP & INFJ Interact, by William D.G. Murray and Rosalie R. Murray (also available on cassette). This neat little book *tells you more about INFJs than anything we've seen,* regardless of the Types with which they frequently interact. But of course, this is primarily an in-depth review of these two Types and how they interact with each other. Includes sections on Love, Sex & Relationships; Attitudes Toward Money; Child-rearing; Recreation & Vacations; INFJ Careers; INFJ Boss with ENFP Employee (and vice-versa); INFJs in Therapy (very helpful information) and more.

OPPOSITES: When ENFP & ISTJ Interact, by William D.G. Murray and Rosalie R. Murray. *Tells you more about ENFPs and more about ISTJs than anything we've* *seen.* Similar topics to ENFP/INFJ above, including Careers for ISTJs and ISTJs in Therapy. Focused on these two Types, but provides useful information for any of the 8 pairs of opposites. Gives both positive and negative aspects, subtle benefits and subtle problems as well as the more obvious ones. Readers' comments: *"Far less expensive than an hour of counseling," "You saved our marriage." "This really helped me understand my boss."*

Discover the Power of Introversion: What Most Introverts Are Never Told, and Extraverts Learn the Hard Way, by Cheryl N. W. Card.
Great little book helps Introverts appreciate themselves (helps Extraverts understand and appreciate Introverts,too). And helps Extraverts recognize the need to develop their own (Introverted) Auxiliary function so they can be whole and effective in day-to-day situations and relationships.

The Way of the Cross: Christian Individuation and Psychological Temperament, by Richard D. Grant, Jr., Ph.D. Grant relates the Jungian typological quaternity and Temperament to the 4 Gospel traditions, the epistles, and numerous Christian traditions including the Angelus, the Eucharist, and the Stations of the Cross. A thoughtful and helpful guide for study, worship and personal growth. Useful for non-Catholics (and even non-Christians) as well as Catholics since his focus is universal, not parochial.

The I Ching: Images of Psychological Typology and Development, by Richard D. Grant, Jr., Ph.D. The ancient Chinese *I Ching*, with 64 symbols (hexagrams) and accompanying text and metaphors, used for ages as an oracle, has a worldview of counterbalanced masculine (yang) and feminine (yin) forces as the basis of all growth and movement. Its advice is timeless, remarkably modern because it is archetypal. Relates the *I Ching* to the 16 Types, 4 Temperaments, archetypes, and Erik Erikson's stages of psychosocial development.

Symbols of Recovery: The 12 Steps at Work in the Unconscious, by Richard D. Grant, Jr., Ph.D.
Explores close connection between the process of recovery (as in the 12-step programs) and the transformation of the deep psyche as explained by both therapeutic modes & spiritual traditions. Correlates the 12-step process with other Symbol Systems that map the spiritual changes deep in the psyche: the "hero's journey" in mythology, the Zodiac, Alchemy processes (symbols used by Jung in therapy) and Tarot cards. Each system is then translated into extremely helpful process questions or exercises based on the 12-steps program.

Making Good Decisions, by Terence Duniho
A brief look at Type & decision-making by groups & individuals.

Your Shadow Side-The Fourth Function: Achilles' Heel and Pearl of Great Price, by Terence Duniho
Recommended reading for all Type people. A very good review of key effects of the energy of our Fourth Function, the vital necessary weakling that gets us into such unexpected trouble, or shows us the way to great spiritual insights. Some worthwhile observations relating to stress, behavior modification, and more.

Personalities at Risk: Addiction, Codependency and Psychological Type, by Terence Duniho
Relates Type/Temperament to addiction and codependency. Useful insights on the importance of the Feeling function in addictive behavior. Describes closed vs. open systems, process addictions and Type, fears and unmet needs, and suggested solutions. A unique contribution.

Wholeness Lies Within: Sixteen Natural Paths Toward Spirituality, by Terence Duniho
Thoughtful volume looks at some of the "Big" questions. Designed "to provide intellectual underpinnings for the person who seeks truth that works, but doesn't want to blindly accept religious dogma" ... and "for the person, like myself, raised with a Judeo- Christian perspective, who up 'til now has not been able to usefully apply that perspective to their own life."

Wellness vs. Neurotic Styles: Holistic vs Monomanic Use of the 4 Functions, by Terence Duniho
We risk potential problems when we fail to develop one of our 4 functions (S, N, T & F). Understanding Type can help us avoid dysfunction in ourselves and misdiagnosis of others. Helps us deal with stress, achieve wellness.

Complete Seminar Presentation Kits for Trainers, Consultants, Educators and Counselors

To present Type to groups, couples, or individual clients, in an organized and professional style
(Overheads, Speaker's script/notes, & Handouts)

Seminar Kit Topics include:
- **Introduction to Psychological Type**
- **Opposites**
- **Type Communication**
- **Type & Teambuilding**
- **Feelers and Thinkers**
- **Type & Careers**
- — and new Seminar Kits based on *Give Yourself the Unfair Advantage,* using Ashleigh Brilliant's famous Pot-Shots™:
- **Give Yourself the Unfair Advantage: Type**— the Brilliant/Murray Introduction to Psychological Type
- **Give Yourself the Unfair Advantage: Temperament**— the Brilliant/Murray Introduction to Psychological Temperament

Workshop & Counseling Materials & Tapes

1. The Type Communications™ Materials – contains 4 materials: (Caveats on Type: Type Basics: Prescriptions for Extraverts (and Introverts, Sensors, et al); When Extravert & Introvert Relate (and E with E; I with I, S with N, etc.) Also available on audiocassette.

2. Reframing - Type, Temperament and Cognitive Therapy. Helps reduce unnecessary conflict.

3. Key Words in Type- for E, I, S, N, T, F, J, & P.

4. Type & Law Office Management- by William D. G. Murray & Frank L. Natter, P.A.- Audiotape & Materials- Helpful for any situation where Client, Staff, and Professional must interact.

5. Type & Case Presentation, William D.G. Murray & Frank L. Natter, P.A. - Audiotape & Materials

6. **Type Speculations on Jury Selection,** Natter & Murray
7. **Energy Flow Templates, - Diagrams of Type Interactions** -William D.G. Murray & Peter Walsh
8. **Type Prayers** by Ellis Harsham
9. **Type Dynamics** by Peter Walsh
10. **Decision-Making from the Dominant Function-** by Peter Walsh
11. **Planning Productive Meetings Using Psychological Type— a Checklist** - Marthanne Luzader
12. **Type-Law Tapes—** 5 tapes by Frank L. Natter, P.A.
13. **Personal Problem-Solving—** 4 tapes by Frank L. Natter, P.A.
14. **Problem-Solving in Relationships** - 3 tapes by Frank L. Natter, P.A.

and by the time you read this, perhaps more...

We also offer an extensive catalogue of Type-related books and materials from other publishers for your convenience.

T&T Inc.'s Training Division offers workshops and training for organizations, couples, and individuals, both in- house and in our facilities.

We will be happy to send you a catalogue or listing of our latest publications and workshops.
Please write to:

Type & Temperament Inc. / Type & Archetype Press

Type & Temperament, Inc
P.O. Box 14285
Charleston SC 29422 USA
TelToll-Free 1-(800) IHS-TYPE
info@typetemperament.com

www: typearchetype.com

Notes